PAINTED BUTTERFLIES

MEMORIES OF A MISSIONARY

FR. CHRISTOPHER FOX, MHM

Fr. Christopher Fox

Copyright © Fr. Christopher Fox
First published in Ireland, in 2015, in co-operation with Choice
Publishing, Drogheda, Co. Louth, Republic of Ireland.
www.choicepublishing.ie

ISBN: 978-1-909154-78-0

Cover design by Michael Gannon.

Dedication:

To my parents, brothers and sisters, family and friends and the many dedicated missionaries with whom I worked.

Table of Contents:

Acknowledgements:

Sincere thanks to all who encouraged me in writing this book and especially to Sean MacCartain whose comments and suggestions I found extremely helpful. Cover design is by Michael Gannon.

Painted Butterflies
(Memories of a Missionary)

Introduction

Ah, the memories that find me, now my hair is turning gray,
Drifting in like painted butterflies from paddocks far away,
Dripping dainty wings of fancy – and the pictures fading fast,
Stand again in rose and purple in the album of the past.
From: *Around the Boree Log* by John O'Brien

I learned these lines as a boy and what seemed rather whimsical then now strikes me with a certain realism. Not only has my hair turned gray but most of it has disappeared. I once had a full head of hair and now when friends poke fun at my bald pate, I claim it is in line with my three planned hair-styles: parted, un-parted and departed!

We all have a story to tell and often the younger generation of my family urge me to write something down of my own life's experiences. The world they live in today is so vastly different from the one I grew up in, that many want to hear those stories and some gently indicate that I'm a sort of the last link with a great distant past. The truth of this will become clearer as I tell the story but here I just note one simple fact for the reader: My grand-father, Owen Fox was born in 1811, over two hundred years ago, when Napoleon was ruling most of Europe. I imagine few people can make such a claim. How come this great span of years? It is strange but true.

Chapter One
My Dad rode with Buffalo Bill

In the fall of 1977, I was preaching in different parishes in the United States under the Missionary co-operative plan, to raise funds for our missionary projects in Africa. My work took me to a parish in Kansas. Missouri. After the Saturday evening Mass, the pastor took me out for a meal and on the way back brought me on a tour of the parish. He pointed out a fine-looking house with a commanding view and said to me. "See that house, Fr. Chris, that house was once owned by William F. Cody. Perhaps you never heard of him? He lived in our parish. Do you know who he was?" I said to him casually, "Not only do I know of him but how would you react if I were to tell you that my Dad once rode with Cody, the famous Buffalo Bill!" Well the pastor didn't quite swerve off the road but exclaimed, "What, surely you mean your grand-father!" "No, my Dad; it's an unusual story. Let me tell you something of it."

In 1887, William F. Cody, Buffalo Bill, the great American showman, who got his name originally because he supplied buffalo meat to the workers building the Kansas railroad, was taking his Wild West Show to Europe. It was a huge spectacle. He wanted to show Europe what the old Wild West was like. There were over 150 Indians including Sitting Bull, the great Sioux chief who wiped out General Custer and his 7th cavalry at the battle of Little Big Horn in 1876. Cody had developed an honest and fair attitude to the Indians and that gained him great respect. The show featured Indian tepees, live buffaloes and Pony Express riders and great displays of horsemanship and shooting. It even re-enacted the battle of Little Big Horn.

Young Mike Fox, my Dad, had gone to Argentina in 1877, ten years before, and was working on a ranch outside Pergamino, some 100 miles west of Buenos Aires He saw a great chance of a trip back to Ireland and getting paid for it. The show, known as the Wild West Exhibition, was to do a seven year tour of six major European cities beginning at the famous Earls Court arena in London. Dad was good with horses and easily got a job as one of the cowboy extras and played his part in the great exhibition. He often spoke of those exploits and meeting so many personalities. He told me that on the last evening of the show in London, Cody himself called him aside to say goodbye. "I know you're leaving us to visit your family in Ireland. Give them my regards" he said. "Don't work this evening, take a seat in my box. Enjoy the show and good luck in your future".

The Homecoming
Dad arrived home to the farm near Killare, Co. Westmeath, on a summer evening while most of the family were out in the fields saving the hay. It was a huge surprise and occasioned a great family party. Neighbours gathered in at night to hear stories from a distant land where so many from Westmeath had settled. At the end of the summer, Dad returned to Argentina. Why had he gone there in the first place?

The Family of Owen Fox and Catherine Kearney
My father's parents, Owen Fox and Catherine Kearney were married in the Church of the Most Holy Redeemer, Ballymore, on 29th July, 1846. The date is significant. 1846 marks the beginning of the great famine in Ireland, the following year being known as 'black 47'. The famine caused by the failure of the potato crop, was to have a devastating effect upon Ireland. Over a million people died of starvation and countless thousands took the 'coffin' ships abroad, to Britain, America, Australia, to any place where there was hope of

survival. Within two generations the population of Ireland was halved, roughly from eight million to four million. Westmeath was not the hardest hit and the locals managed to survive on other meagre crops from the land. In fact some people came to the midlands to get help. Two young Tipperary men, almost dying of hunger, found their way to Killeenbrack and were glad to get some food from my grandfather as they waited for a chance to get a boat to America. For the vast majority of young men and women in the country there was only one way to survive and that was to take the emigrant ship. Before the famine, Moate and surrounding area had a population of over 13,000. In 1847 there were over a hundred baptisms in Ballymore parish alone. The annual figure today is about twenty.

The origin of the name FOX is interesting. It came to be used as the regular surname for an ancient Celtic family called O'Catharnaigh. Back in the 11th century one of the O'Catharnaigh chieftains was given the nickname An Sionnach (The Fox) either because he had red hair or perhaps had some wily traits of character. The soubriquet became traditional in the family and in the course of time it supplanted the original family name O'Catharnaigh and eventually became the recognised surname. The Celtic FOX trace their descent from Maine. son of Niall of the Nine Hostages, King of Ireland in 397. The original territory of the Sionnach (Fox) clan was located in Westmeath and Offaly. The clan was displaced following the Cromwellian wars and their descendants were scattered and became tenants-at-will under the Cromwellian landlords.

It was in the midst of the doom and gloom of the famine that my grandparents exchanged their married vows. Catherine Kearney was from Ballymore. Her brother, Thomas, was ordained priest in Maynooth in June of that year, 1846. He served many years in the diocese of Meath. His last assignment was parish priest of Bohermeen where he died in 1889. Owen Fox had a modest farm of about 60 acres, near Killare and the Hill of Uisneagh in the barony of Rathconrath which had been a centre of considerable importance from prehistoric right down to late medieval times.

Their eldest child, Alexander, was born exactly a year after their marriage and was baptised on 30th July 1847. Michael, my father, was their ninth child. In all my grandparents had 18 children. Four died in infancy; 14 lived to adulthood. Most married and some had large families. There were 65 grand-children in all, myself the youngest of the lot. (see appendix for details of the family tree)

Emigration to Argentina.

Seven of the first eight children, five sons and two daughters, on reaching adulthood emigrated, James to Australia and the other six, including my father, to Argentina. After the famine, as already noted, there was huge emigration from Ireland, mostly to English speaking countries such as Britain, USA and Australia. Most found work in the industrial cities of these countries. Strong Irish communities were formed in the cities of Liverpool, Birmingham, Boston, Chicago, New York, Melbourne and Sydney. Argentina was the big exception, a non English speaking country where the immigrants found work on the land.

The Irish connection with Argentina goes back to the early 19th century. Argentina won independence from Spain in 1816. Admiral William Brown from Foxford, Co. Mayo, played a prominent part and is honoured as the founder of the Argentine navy. Another man, Thomas O'Brien from Co. Wicklow was adjutant to San Martin, the hero of the war of Independence. It is said that San Martin begged O'Brien to bring out people from Ireland to develop Argentina, a country of vast unclaimed lands.

O'Brien had no success in his own county Wicklow. Then he met John Mooney of Streamstown, Co. Westmeath. John's sister Mary was married to Patrick Bookey and the three of them accompanied O'Brien when he returned to Argentina in 1828. They achieved rapid success in farming. They wrote home to Ireland telling of the great opportunities available and inviting people to come out. That was the beginning of the exodus from Westmeath and Longford to Argentina. A small percentage also emigrated there from Wexford, Cork and Clare.

After the famine, the number from Westmeath and Longford greatly increased. This was mainly due to the influence of an Irish Dominican priest, Fr. Anthonio Fahy who was based in Argentina. When he came home to Ireland on leave his message was, "Come to Argentina, you are from the land and in Argentina good land is going for a song; work, save and buy". Many followed his advice, including my Dad, his three brothers and two sisters. Alexander and John were the first to go together with Mary and Brigid. Eugene (Owen) and Michael (my Dad) joined them later. Fr. Fahy, whose memory is greatly honoured to this day in Argentina, acted as godfather, work organiser, spiritual mentor, match-maker, the lot. Today, an area west of Buenos Aires as big as Ireland is populated mostly by the descendants of these Irish immigrants who found a new home so far away. Even to this day they speak Spanish with a definite touch of a Westmeath accent! Family names such as McDonnell, Geoghegan, Mahon, Brown, Moran and Nugent are very common.

I often think of my Dad, a young man of nineteen, travelling to Liverpool in the fall of 1877, to catch a tramp steamer for the long voyage to Argentina. His passage was paid and he told me he had three sovereigns in his pocket. True he was joining his brothers in a distant land but it took a fair measure of courage to face such an uncertain future. The parting must have been difficult for the parents, especially the mother? As each of their children reached adulthood they set off for a distant land. At least Thomas, the second son, remained at home to help on the farm and there were young brothers and sisters to be taken care of. My Dad never spoke much to me of his father but he told me many stories of his mother whom he dearly loved and whom he considered to be a saint. He once told me that despite having to care for her big family she said the 15 decades of the Rosary every day.

Michael Fox reached Argentina after a six weeks voyage. He was met by his brothers who helped him to settle down quickly. He got a job working for a local rancher. His brothers were already making their mark. Alexander acquired land and eventually became a successful sheep farmer. He married Catherine Rafferty and had four sons. He died in 1921. Later on his family moved first to Venezuela and later to the USA. Owen (Eugene) became a very successful cattle rancher and played a big part in the social affairs of the large Irish community. He married Catherine Tobin in 1898. My Dad was best man at the wedding. They had three daughters and one son. He died in 1940. I was in regular contact with his grandson, Denis Eugene McDonnell-Fox and his family until Denis passed away in 2010. Of the others, the two girls never married nor returned to Ireland. Mary died in 1929 and Brigid in 1937. John, my other uncle there returned to Ireland and settled down in Dysart, outside Mullingar. He married twice and raised ten children. (For family details see Appendix)

Early Adventures

Dad had many stories of his early days in Argentina. Shortly after his arrival, he got a job on a farm. The first thing to buy was a horse, often the only means of transport. When he got his next pay packet he rode into Pergamino, a town some twenty miles from the ranch where he worked. He had plenty of shopping to do. He bought some work clothes, a big hat, some tobacco as he smoked a pipe and some toiletries. He noticed a sinister looking character following him about but did not think much of it. However some few miles out on the way home, his horse making good time with a loping gentle gallop which it could sustain for many miles, Dad heard the sound of hooves gaining up on him. He looked back and saw it was the man who had followed him around in Pergamino. Dad felt that he was up to no good. He knew that many of these natives carried knives for robbery. They were scared only of pistols which some gringos (foreigners) carried. Dad had nothing except his wits and a large clay pipe. He pulled his big hat down low, buttoned up his jacket and bulged his fist with the pipe inside giving the impression of a gun. The stranger drew alongside, friendly enough and asked what he had in his hand. Dad ignored him completely, but his body language said, "You just try something and you'll find out". They passed a discarded item on the trail; it was an old saddle. The stranger said, "That would be useful for you. Why don't you stop and pick it up?". Dad kept silent as they rode side by side. Twice the stranger tried to jostle his horse and Dad gave him a threatening look. After a few more miles, the stranger lost his nerve and turned around and rode back. Dad's bluff had paid off. Years after Dad had died, a local neighbour, old Joe Fay, asked me if I had heard the story of how my father had held off the bandits. No, I said, genuinely interested in a story I hadn't heard. Only when he was well into it did I realise it was the same story except now there was a gang of them. The pulled-down hat and the imitation gun were the same. I began to wonder how it would end. No way would these bandits turn round and run without good reason. True to form, it had a great ending. They were about to enter a narrow path among trees and it was getting dark. They were already fingering their knives. Joe concluded the story: "Your Dad knew that it was here they had planned the ambush. At the last moment, he spurred his horse forward, stood up on the stirrups and in the semi-darkness, pulled out his big pipe like a gun and waving it in the air shouted: 'This is a dangerous place, boys, if you've guns, you'd better draw them!' and before this dangerous gunman the bandits fled like leaves before the Autumn wind". A much better story and why change it?

The haunted house

Dad who was sceptical of all ghost stories used to love telling another story to highlight how some could originate. When leaving Ireland he was told by his mother to look up old Joe Mahon who had emigrated many years before and had never come home. In due course Dad enquired about his whereabouts and was told he lived in a little cottage about ten miles away, doing odd jobs for a local farmer. "A bit odd but a kind old soul" he was told. One summer evening Dad rode over to call on him and give him greetings from Ireland. He had no difficulty finding the little flat roofed house and as he was passing the window he saw the old man kneeling before the open hearth frying some meat on a pan over the open fire. There was a kettle hanging on a small crane over the fire. Dad saw a long piece of stiff wire outside the door and on the spur of the moment, he grabbed it, leaped on to the roof and looked down the chimney. He saw the old man leaning over the pan turning the meat over. It was a simple trick to put a hook on the wire, lower it gently down the chimney, grab the kettle and haul it up. The result was more than he had bargained for. The old man let a roar out him, ran from the house and hid in an old shed some distance away.

Dad hurried down; the joke was over; he tried to explain and apologise but as soon as the old man saw him, he caught him by the arm, pulled him aside and warned him. "Young man, I don't know where you're from, but for God's sake, don't go near that house. That house is 'ghosted'. With my own eyes I saw the kettle go right up the chimney". Dad had some explaining to do and even in the end the old man was not quite convinced.

Pondering the future, Argentina or Ireland?

Life was uneventful enough. The Buffalo Bill episode was the highlight of adventure and when Dad returned to Argentina in the fall of 1887, he settled down to routine work on a farm and continued there for several years He worked for a wealthy land owner, was saving good money and pondering his future. Now in his early forties; it was time for him to settle down and get married, but where? In Argentina or return to Ireland? Events back home settled the question. Dad's father had died rather young in 1879. Thomas, the second son, who was running the farm died suddenly in 1899. The following year Dad got the call from his mother. "Come home, the farm is yours." He was out ploughing with oxen when he got word. He was delighted, wound up his affairs, said good-bye to his brothers, sisters and many friends and headed for Ireland in early 1900. Many years later we found an old Argentina coin of that date in the garden at home.

Back in the Old Country, marriage, children and bereavement.

Ireland in the early 20th century was a poor country. Agitation over land reform and Home Rule was prominent. The farm near Killare, about 60 acres used for mixed farming, (some farm animals and agriculture) provided a reasonable livelihood. In 1906, Dad was now in his 48th year and decided to take the plunge. In February of that year he married Brigid Scally from Ballymore. In due time three children arrived, Owen born in 1907, Ellen in 1910 and Alexander in 1911. Brigid's health was not the best and sadly she passed away after the birth of Alexander in 1911. Dad's mother whom he idolised passed away the same year. So he was left a very lonely grieving man with three young children to look after. As is usual in rural Ireland, the family stepped in to help. His brother Christy who was married to Kate Cuskelly and had a farm in nearby Glascorn took Ellen. His brother, Peter, with a farm and shop in Churchtown near Ballynacargy, had married Elizabeth Leavy in 1905 and he took Owen, while his sister, Anne, who had married Owen Cowley of Cloonagh near Ballinagore also in 1905, took Alexander.

Owen went to St. Finian's College in Mullingar and in 1924 emigrated to the USA. He worked hard, survived the great depression of '29 by getting a job as a taxi driver. He married Bridie O'Leary from Co. Kerry and had four sons. He came back to Ireland on a visit in the summer of 1949, when I met him for the first time. Ellen, or Nellie as she was known, made her permanent home in Glascorn with Uncle Christy. In 1940 she married Hugh Whelan. They had a daughter, Marie, the following year and everybody was so happy. Then tragedy struck. Nellie developed cancer and died within a year, leaving her husband Hugh heartbroken with a baby daughter to look after. Marie grew up to be a beautiful, vivacious young woman. I officiated at her marriage to Sean McGowan of Blackrock, Dublin in 1968. They had two sons. Then tragedy struck again. Marie developed cancer in 1974 and despite the best medical help died one year later. The two sons grew up to be fine young men. The younger, Alan, distinguished himself in rugby, playing outhalf for Blackrock, Leinster and Ireland. The third of Dad's first family, Alexander, or Alick as he was known, was reared in Cloonagh, had a bad accident to his leg which left him with a severe limp. He returned to the family home in Killeenbrack He never married and later emigrated to England where he died of a heart attack in 1965.

In 1918, Dad was now a widower for seven years. He was in constant touch with his three children as their welfare was his main concern. He was approaching his 60th birthday, in perfect health and thinking of his future. Why not get married again? His younger brother Peter encouraged him. In fact he could easily arrange a meeting with a very suitable partner, the daughter of one of his customers, Tom Mulvany, from Paddenstown nearby. Mary Jane Mulvany, a beautiful woman of 29 was the support and home-keeper of her father, who had been married twice and had lost both wives. Mary Jane was anxious to find a home of her own and have a family and Michael Fox, though senior in age, was a splendid gentleman with a farm of his own. After several meetings when he proposed, she gladly accepted. But there was a problem. Her father refused to give his permission and blessing. He was thinking of his own interests. Only at the last did he relent and the marriage took place in St. Matthew's Church, Milltown, on 5th June, 1918. After the modest celebrations, they returned to the farmhouse in Killeenbrack, Streamstown, to begin their married life together.

Some sixty years later, after I had conducted a funeral service at that church in Milltown, a man pushed his way through the crowd to greet me. He told me his name, Ned Seery, which meant nothing to me. Neither did his subsequent ramblings about how he had been a Mass server in this church as a boy when times were poor. He had served at many funerals and only one wedding. Then he really got my attention when he said, "That was the wedding of your parents." He described my mother, such a lovely woman, arriving in a jaunting car and my Dad, a senior figure, waiting at the altar for her. He finished by saying, "I always knew they had a son a priest and I felt I had some claim on you for I served your parents' wedding Mass." Suddenly the little church was transformed for me. I knelt at the altar, imagined the scene and gave thanks to God for such wonderful parents. I thanked Ned Seery, the one time Mass server and invited him to attend my Silver Jubilee the following year.

Chapter Two
The Family and Boyhood Memories.

After the wedding in Milltown church on 5th June, 1918, Michael Fox took his young bride, Mary Jane Mulvany to the family homestead in Killeenbrack, Streamstown, near Killare and the hill of Uisneagh. The home would not be too different from the one Mary Jane had left in Paddenstown. There was a kitchen with open hearth, a modest sitting room and a bedroom off the kitchen, with a couple of rooms upstairs, no running water but a pump in the yard. A paraffin lamp was essential as rural electrification was still forty years away. So all the electrical appliances which we take for granted today in the household were just non existent. There was no TV, radio or phone. The weekly paper *The Westmeath Examiner* was the main source of local news with some national news included. Ramblers to the house exchanged stories. The Sunday Mass was a great social occasion not only for worship but for after Mass discussions. Furniture in the house was sparse, a few simple chairs, an armchair near the fire where Dad usually sat as he told us stories, a dresser with crockery stacked up, *speckled and white and blue and brown.* as described in Padraig Colum's *Old Woman of the Roads.* It was fairly typical of the farmhouses of the day.

I often wonder what were my parents' thoughts and hopes as they settled down to married life together, a fifty nine year old man and his twenty nine year old bride. They could hardly have foreseen that they would be blest with almost forty years together with six children and nineteen grand-children and that some thirty seven years later their youngest son would be ordained to the priesthood and offer Mass of Thanksgiving in their family home.

Their six children consisted of three girls and three boys, arriving in the sequence of girl, boy, girl, boy, girl, boy, described by one wit as a neat piece of family planning! The eldest born on 22nd March, 1919, was christened Catherine and as with all of us she attended Boher national school. Early on she felt a call to the religious life. She joined the Little Sisters of the Assumption whose work is caring for poor families often living in deprived areas of large cities. She left home in September 1938. I remember the morning well as I tried to hold back the tears as she set off for London where she would begin her formation. During the early years of the war she spent most nights in the basement of the convent sheltering from the awful German blitz. After making her final profession she qualified as a nurse. She was not to get home again till 1948. She gave a lifetime of service to the poor in London, Birmingham, Liverpool, Edinburgh and Gateshead. Eventually in her eighties she came back to Ireland and retired in the house of the Congregation in Finglas, Dublin. She is now 95, still alert and well looked after in St. Monica's Home in Belvidere Place, Dublin.

The second child, Thomas, (baptised Thomas Ashe after the Irish patriot who died in 1917) was born in 1920. He looked after the farm and was my main support during my long training for the priesthood. He did a stint in the States where he met his future wife, Delia Kelly, from Co. Roscommon. They married in 1966, returned to the home place and had two children, Mary Geralyn and Michael. Sadly in March 1983 Tom died at the relatively young age of 62 and Delia died four years later. It was a tragic blow for their two children but they came through it well. Their daughter, Mary, married Terry Healy from Rosemount. They have two children, Thomas and Jane, both now adults and doing well in their chosen careers. Michael, unmarried, continues to live in Killeenbrack.

The third child of my parents was born in March, 1922, and was christened Mary Jane. A very devout woman, she tried out her religious vocation and decided it was not for her. She married Michael Carton of Horseleap in 1953. They had five children, four daughters and one son, Mary Frances, Brigid, Patrick, Margaret and Catherine.

Michael was the fourth child, born in July, 1924. He grew up tall and strong and was a gifted footballer. Jobs wee scarce in Ireland and he emigrated to the United States in 1950 and settled in New York. In 1954 he married Peggy Kelly from Rathconrath. They raised six children, Mary, Margaret, Michael, Kathleen, Teresa and Kevin. Again sadly in December, 1983, Michael died at the relatively young age of 59.

My sister Teresa was born on 2nd October, 1926. She qualified as a confectioner and worked in Edwards in Dublin. In 1951 she married Benny Moran from Navan. They had six children, Michael, Aidan, Bernard, Colin, Imelda and Sean. Benny ran a very successful furniture business. When this was wound up the family branched out on their own and continue to run a most successful company.

I was the last of my parents' six children, born when my Dad was 72 year and Mum was 42 so I must have caught the last bus out of that heavenly terminus. I arrived on the 8th April, 1931. As with the others, I was delivered in my parents' bedroom in the small farmhouse. A good neighbour, Mrs Scally, acted as midwife. I was often told of the joy when my first whimpering was heard. I was baptised a few days later by Fr. Casey, the Parish priest of Ballymore. What name would I be called? It was normal to stick to traditional family names. I had an uncle Christy, living in nearby Glascorn and an uncle Peter in Churchtown, so they settled for Christopher Peter.

The youngest in the family is supposed to be spoiled but I have little memory of that although I'm told my sisters vied for the dubious honour of carrying me around! Life in the country in the thirties in Ireland was anything but luxurious. Living on a farm we had the basics required and none of us went hungry. But we were all called upon to play our part in the household chores and outside on the farm, bringing in the cows, counting the sheep, fetching water from the pump, collecting eggs when the hens laid them in the outhouses, weeding the turnip and carrot drills in the garden, picking the potatoes sometimes on frosty mornings and running errands to the local shop. We had fun and games too. In winter we enjoyed snowball fights and sliding across frozen pools,

My first day at Boher national school was 3rd October, 1936. I remember vividly the details of that day, the journey across the fields with my siblings, joined by other children, the stop at the pump in Ballalavin for a long cool drink of water, then the final few hundred yards to the old school. I can still get the smell of musty damp overcoats in the hallway, the rush to the small classrooms when the bell rang. Master Kavanagh greeted me and gave me a penny. Miss Fitzimons, who was in charge of the lower classes, did likewise. Two pennies, I felt rich.

The two classrooms were in poor condition, but we crowded in as best we could. There was promise of a new school but times were hard and money was scarce. However mostly through the great efforts of the parish priest, Fr. Mulvany, and the generosity of the local people, enough was collected to begin the project and in due time the new school was completed. The formal opening and blessing took place on 18th June, 1940. I remember the day well, the transfer from the old crowded classrooms to the brand new classrooms, the bright walls, the smell of fresh paint, the gleaming desk-tops as yet spotless from any ink blots and the large windows. We jostled for places around the teacher's desk, now being used as an altar, as Fr. Mulvany said Mass and later went round blessing all the classrooms.

When Mass was over, the altar became the teacher's desk again. Pupils' desks were put in line and our schooling continued in these new congenial surroundings. Master Kavanagh and Miss Fitzimons did their best to bring us the treasures of wisdom and knowledge, with limited success. Corporal punishment was part of the culture of the day and I sometimes got a few cane-slaps of the best but we boys took it in our stride. Compared to some other schools it was applied with certain moderation. We played games in the small playground. There was the occasional bout of fisticuffs among us when tempers flared. The sudden appearance of the Master put a dampening effect on all such outbursts.

The years passed, not exactly the happiest times of my life but we survived. During the winter months traipsing across the fields to school in snow and frost was not easy. We always welcomed springtime and on 1st May, we discarded our shoes and raced with abandon across the fields barefooted.

A new church

Now that we had a new school the whole focus of the parish was on a new church as the old church was in poor shape. The parish priest, Fr. Christopher Casey, a well beloved pastor, had collected some money for the purpose. He had served the parish well and was now in his eighties. He used to arrive for Mass on Sunday mornings being driven in an old Model T Ford that seldom exceeded ten miles an hour. One Sunday coming down the altar steps at the end of Mass he stumbled and fell. Parishioners rushed to help. It was his last Mass in Boher. He died on 1st June, 1939. He was a staunch nationalist. He is remembered too for his attitude to time. He never accepted summer time as he didn't believe God's order should be tampered with. Even old time had to be according to the sun and that meant twenty five minutes past the hour GMT. So in the summer from Mullingar to Ballymore we had three times, new time, old time and Fr. Casey's time, much to the amusement and sometimes confusion of visitors!

Fr. Casey was succeeded by Fr. Patrick Mulvany who determined to push ahead with the building of a new church. A site was donated nearby and on 1sst February, 1940, the feast of St. Brigid, the ground was blest by the bishop of Meath, the first sod was cut and work commenced. Despite the difficulty of the war years, through the inspiration of Fr. Mulvany and with great support from parishioners, the contractor, Bernard McEntagart from Navan, was able to finish the work in good time. The church was formally opened and blest on 9th November, 1941. It was dedicated to St. Brigid who had founded the first church in this area some 1,500 years previously. I served Mass in this church during my school years. It was here I said my first Mass and celebrated many happy occasions. Despite long absences on the missions I always felt I was coming home when I came to Boher.

The Hill of Uisneagh

We lived near Killare which nestles in the shadow of the hill of Uisneagh. I roamed across this hill many times as a boy without realising its historical significance. It covers a wide range of land and it rises to six hundred feet above sea level, the highest point in the midlands. There are magnificent views from the top. It is claimed that on a clear day one can see the O'Connell monument in Glasnevin, Dublin. One can certainly see the vast expanse of the Shannon river near Athlone and locations in far away counties. Uisneagh was the seat of the High Kings of Ireland before Tara. A famous landmark on the side of the hill is Ail na Mireann, (the stone of divisions), a massive thirty ton rock, commonly called the Cat Stone or the Cat Rock where the five ancient provinces of Ireland met. Circling the great rock is an attractive earthen bank which archaeologists claim identifies it as a prehistoric burial place probably dating back to 2000 BC.

When the druids were the religious leaders they celebrated the feast of Bealtine (summer festival) with great ceremonial fires and dances on Uisneagh. That was the signal for other sacred fires to be lit on surrounding hills near and far, on Knockastia near Rosemount, on Croghan Hill in Offaly and right across the country. In the 5th century St. Patrick came here and formed a Christian community to end the reign of the druids. A large rectangular stone at the top of the hill is called St. Patrick's Bed as he is reputed to have slept there.

St. Brigid's Well (Bride's Well)

Killare was once an important place and was closely associated with St. Brigid. One tradition claims that she received the religious veil from St. Hugh on Uisneagh. She certainly established a church and convent in Killare. Long after they fell into ruins, a nearby holy well, called St. Brigid's Well, continued to attract many pilgrims. Strangely the day of gathering there was Good Friday. Many came to do the stations of the Cross around the fourteen flat stones placed around the well. My mother took me there on more that one occasion. One of the flagstones had a distinct imprint of a fish's tail on it. Legends abound about how this happened and about the miraculous cure of a baby in 1920 when placed in the water. There are not many pilgrims today but the site has been repaired and renovated in recent times by local volunteers and it stands as a fitting reminder of the great saint who came here towards the end of the 5th century, St. Brigid, Mary of the Gael.

The L.D.F.

Many dates from my boyhood years are still vivid in my mind. In September 1939 I remember my brother Tom announcing that the war in Europe had started. A year later Master Kavanagh informed us before class one morning that Germany had invaded Holland and Belgium. Political speeches were often given outside churches after Mass on Sunday and I recall Erskine Childers, our local T.D. telling us that the German forces were now just forty miles from Moscow. To us it all seemed so far away. There was talk that Germany might invade Ireland as a means of attacking Britain, so a local security force, a sort of Home Guard, was formed in many areas. In Boher, a company was formed with Master Tom Kavanagh as leader and Paddy McKenna as his assistant. Its duty was to patrol the roads at night and to erect poles in large level fields to prevent possible plane landings. In 1942 the name given was the Local Defence Force (LDF). My brother, Mike, joined at the start and I used to admire his green uniform and shiny new boots and leggings.

Master Kavanagh was company commander but 50 men were needed to form a company and having roped in any local male he could find he was still one short. One morning in school he came to my desk, told me to stand up and asked me how old I was. It was 7th April, 1943 and I told him proudly that I would be 12 the following day. "You're a big lad," he said, "I'll put you down as 16". So he enrolled me in the LDF a day short of my twelfth birthday to defend my country. The Master took me to the spare classroom where all the military gear was kept and I was duly rigged out with pants, tunic, cap, boots and leggings and even a great coat. I was so excited. My parents got a surprise that evening when I arrived home with my new uniform and proudly told them that I had joined the L.D.F. My father was utterly tolerant in such matters as he felt the Master knows best.

Wednesday was our night for drill. I would rush home from school, discard my short pants and don my full military uniform. I enjoyed the whole experience. I was a boy in an adult world. An army commandant used to come from Athlone and we were drilled and we marched and I sometimes even got to carry a rifle. I remember shooting practice at targets set up against Clare Hill. One had to graduate from a .22 rifle to a Winchester or Lee Enfield. I made the grade but the Winchester was far too heavy for me. The report of each shot and the recoil were dreadful. I was so glad of the order: "Adopt the prone position." I could now rest the rifle on a mound of earth, with my elbows on the ground and take careful aim at the target over a hundred yards away. We had four shots each. I was proud of my achievement, two bulls, an inner and an outer, thirteen points out of a possible sixteen. We were in rows of five and when the firing stopped, the commandant roared, "Is everybody finished?" The man on the ground beside me, Johnny Hegarty. shouted "This damn thing won't go off at all". The commandant looked down, "Why you idiot, can't you see the safety catch is still on". The commandant leaned down and released the catch while Johnny's finger was still on the trigger. There was a mighty report from the gun and the bullet hit the ground ten yards away. Nobody was hurt. We all laughed. Come on, Mr. Hitler, we're ready for you.

We marched in Boher on St. Patrick's Day. On that occasion I forsook my altar-boy's role to don a different uniform and attended Mass in the gallery clutching my rusty .22 rifle. We marched in Athlone on Easter Monday and we seemed to be part of a vast army of marching men and military bands from all over Ireland. It was a spectacular occasion. The marching ended and we were given a meal in the open. This was followed by a football match between an army team and one drawn from the combined LDF. Then we dispersed and many sought extra sustenance in the local pubs.

Our transport was due to leave for home at six o'clock. A big open cattle truck had conveyed the contingents from Boher, Ballymore and Rosemount to Athlone that morning, all standing, packed tightly. As we assembled for the return journey, it was obvious that many had taken more drink than was good for them. A few were well oiled, as they say. We climbed aboard and started home. Coming towards Moate, a row broke out. I could hear some rough language and blows were exchanged but we were all too tightly packed for any sort of fight! I kept near my big brother, Mike, up at the front. The truck stopped outside the police barracks in Moate, the driver hoping to calm things down a bit. Instead I remember one burley fellow jumping off the truck, banging on a window of the barracks and defying any garda to come out and fight him! We moved on. I was at the front, overlooking the windscreen above the driver. A big fellow pushed past me, reeking of beer. He leaned down and banged on the windscreen in front of the driver. He obviously wanted to relieve nature. I remember vividly his words: "Stop this effing truck or I'll brain you as sure as Jesus will judge you!" (He used a rather broad form of the Holy Name). In all my years of ministry, I haven't heard a finer proclamation of the last judgement!

When the Rosemount contingent got off I thought that would ease the tension. Instead there was now more room to fight. I heard blows and one man fell off the truck somewhere near Bishopstown. We stopped. There was general confusion. Some of us had had enough. We jumped off and we decided to walk home from there, just another three miles or so. I was with two others as far as the Lodge in Mosstown. Then I made my own way home, past Killians, up Ballinivea hill, past Mentons, then across some fields by moonlight to our old farmhouse. I could see the paraffin lamp inside. I rushed in the door, bursting with excitement, wanting to share the events of the day. My mother and father were alone in the kitchen on their knees saying the Rosary. My mother looked up. "You're late," she said, "where have you been all this time? Now say the last decade... Our Father..." What an anti-climax, and then the thought of returning to the humdrum of school life when Easter was over.

The nightly journeys

Countless other memories crop up. Dad liked to visit his brothers and other relatives. He used to take me with him as he needed me to hold the lantern when coming back at night. We travelled by pony and trap. The visits to uncle Peter in Churchtown were the most pleasant as he had a shop and usually gave me a few sweets. Neighbours would drop in for a chat, most of them in their senior years. I usually sat in a corner, bored to death and reading an old comic book for the fifth time and listening to these old men talking about Parnell, the War of Independence and the Civil War, Collins and De Valera. The sinking of the Titanic seemed just yesterday's news to some of them. Indeed, Pat Fox, a neighbour of my dad but no relation, had perished in the tragedy. Sometimes before leaving one of them might notice this little lad in the corner. The conversation went like this. To my Dad, "Mike is that really your little boy?" I can still see the glint in my Dad's eye as coming over and tousling my hair, he would say with pride, "Yes indeed, this is my youngest. He's the scrapings of the pot!" I was mortified. Apparently after the famine in Ireland the youngest was often called either the shakings of the bag or the scrapings of the pot! What a title.

We would often return home at the dead of night, with me holding the lantern, and Dad telling me stories of South America and recounting some marvellous ghost stories as we slowly made our way along lonely country roads. There were ghostly carriages and headless horsemen sweeping down the fields of Meerscourt and many weird figures among the moonlight shadows. Strangely enough I was never very afraid. After all, Dad was there and he'd often put a protective arm around me. A strong relationship grew between us which greatly shaped my future outlook and character, a boy of eight and a father who was eighty. I had a father and grand-father rolled into one. Dad was not overtly religious but he was steeped in Celtic spirituality, the goodness of a loving God and the beauty of all creation. I learned so much of Christian values from him and from my mother who was much more devotional, very strict in the practice of religion but overall was inclined to worry about too many things.

A Day at the threshing

At harvest time, the big day of the threshing was a great occasion. We took the day off school and waited for Hugh Clavin to come with the tractor and the big threshing mill. Many neighbours came each with his job to do, pitching the sheaves, cutting the binding twine, feeding the mill, collecting the wheat or oats or barley, tying the bags. There were plenty of jobs for boys to do and we rushed around caught up in the hurley-burley of the day. Occasionally a rat might bolt from the stack to add to the excitement. The poet Patrick Kavanagh describes the marvellous day of the threshing in one of his poems "Tarry Flynn".

Mullingar

Trips to the town of Mullingar were a real treat. Before Christmas, when the turkeys were sold, my mother always took me on Hanlon's bus. It was exciting seeing the electric lights, the Christmas decorations, buying Christmas goods, especially my new shoes which would have to last for a full year. Before leaving town there was always the visit to the Cathedral. I can still see my mother's face in the dim light as she knelt in prayer before the Crib near the High Altar. Even to a distracted boy more interested in toys and sports, there was a deep impression of a wider world, a spiritual world which touched all our lives.

Fair Days

Occasionally, my big brother, Mike, took me to the fair in Moate or Mullingar, if we had a few animals for sale. It was a sight to see such an ocean of animals crowding the main street. There were no cattle marts in those days. I would watch the ritual of buying and selling, the bargaining, the handshakes, the luck pennies demanded, the deals closed. If there was no sale, farmers had to drive the animals back home Once at a pig fair in Ballymore we had four pigs for sale and there was little interest. My brother, Mike, got fed up, told me to take them home with the horse and cart and he went off on his bike. As I passed a farmer's house on the way home the owner stopped me and asked what I was doing. I told him we had failed to sell. He offered to buy one of the pigs and asked how much. After much haggling we agreed on a price. On reaching home minus one of the pigs, Dad was afraid I had lost it. When I produced the money he was so proud that his boy of ten could handle such a situation and told everybody about it.

Imagination

There were few books in the house although we all liked reading. In pre-electricity days we depended on the paraffin lamp at night. My brother, Mike, used to get some cowboy books and I enjoyed reading them. The wild west became a real place for me and one's imagination can do the rest. When riding the cart horse down from the high field, I wasn't just a boy doing a job, I was the last of the Texas Rangers out in search of baddies. When I took the mare and cart out to bring fodder to the cattle, I was no farm hand. I was riding shotgun on the Pony Express delivering mail in bandit country. Ah! the wonder of a vivid imagination.

Such are my boyhood memories of growing in the thirties and early forties. They were difficult times for many people. Few pupils from rural Ireland got a chance of a secondary education. To find work after primary school was the real challenge, otherwise emigration. During the war there was rationing of tea and sugar and many items. There were no fruits such as bananas or oranges, no chocolate and few sweets. Yet growing up on a farm had its own advantages. We had a churn and could produce our own supply of great tasting butter. No chef could improve on the flavour of freshly dug new potatoes, boiled over the turf fire, mashed and served with a pinch of salt and butter. From time to time we killed a pig and that gave rise to great feasting on fresh fillets of pork, black puddings and giblets and one cannot forget the culinary delights of pig's head and crubeens (trotters) After a killing some neighbours would come and collect portions of the newly slaughtered animal. The pig would be carved up and the large sides would be salted and thus preserved to last us during the coming year.

For years we had no radio. I would go to a neighbour's house to listen to Michael O'Hehir on All Ireland Sunday. When we did get a radio it required a dry battery and a heavy wet battery which had to be charged regularly in Mullingar where there was electric power. I have memories of riding my bicycle home from town carrying the heavy battery in one hand and trying to negotiate my way along some poor roads, often of a wet evening.

For local entertainment we had football and hurling matches and parish rivalries were often keen. Boher hall was a great centre for dances and as the bicycle was the common mode of transport I remember seeing hundreds of bicycles piled up outside. During Lent quite a few excellent plays were staged there as the Rural Drama Movement was quite strong at the time. A big race meeting was organised locally and it was a very exciting day for all of us pupils, free from school and watching not only the horses but the many dubious entertainers. I saw a three-card-trick man relieving a poor customer of all his money in less than five minutes. Lilliput sports on the shores of Lough Ennell was an annual event with boat rides and endless amusement games.

At home neighbours would call in some evenings and tell stories or organise a game of cards, mostly penny 45s! Mrs Menton, our neighbour, acquired a new machine called a gramaphone. She brought it over to our house one evening and played records of songs by John McCormack and Delia Murphy and many others. I was allowed to wind up the machine after each record.

Looking back on those years now I remember the wonderful people in the area, good neighbours ready to help in any necessity. There were some well-known characters too. Moll and Matt Casey were great sources of news and gossip. Moll had a sharp tongue so it was better to keep in her good books. Matt took great pleasure in finding out secrets. I remember him once boasting excitedly that he had found out who the 'mystery' man was. He was referring to a stranger who was beginning to court a local girl. As someone who liked to dramatise simple events, one night he got a shock himself. He was walking home from the pub in Streamstown. It was near midnight and when passing Boher he was surprised to see the lights were on in the church. The road approaching his house in Balliniva is low lying with a gateway off it leading to a couple of houses. It was called the haunted gate. As Matt walked slowly home along this road he began to discern the outline of a vehicle approaching slowly. He stopped and stared. No he hadn't too much to drink. He wasn't dreaming. Coming towards him slowly was a hearse with the parking lights on. Behind it he could see the outline of some figures walking.. Matt nearly fainted. "My God, I'm ghosted," he cried. He jumped the hedge and raced home across some fields. He rushed in the door, shouting, "Moll, Moll, the Holy Water, get the Holy Water, I've seen a ghost. It may be after me. I may be going to die!" When Moll calmed him down she gave him the explanation. A neighbour up the road, Paddy Connell, an old bachelor living alone had died quite suddenly that evening. A neighbour sent for the parish priest and the undertaker. As he had no relatives it was decided that there would be no wake in the house. The body after due preparation should be put in the coffin and taken to the church. The parish priest said the prayers for the dead and sent word to the church caretaker to leave the church open with the lights on. It was near midnight when they were ready to leave. The journey was only about a mile. A few neighbours walked slowly after the hearse, saying the Rosary. It was this scene which accosted Matt on his way home from the pub. It could not have been better staged managed.

A neighbour of ours, Stephen Daly, loved to put on airs and graces. He had a farm nearby and often claimed he couldn't really get down to work till he had sorted out the morning's mail. The most he ever got was a card at Christmas. When he ran out of a shilling or two when playing cards he would casually ask if anyone present could cash a cheque for a thousand dollars which he had just received from a company in the States for some consultancy work!

The Wrinkle brothers, Pat and Joe, ran the forge near the school. It was always exciting to visit the forge and watch the blacksmiths at work shoeing the horses. We were often chased out of the place as the nuisance which we were but sometimes I was allowed to use the bellows to stoke up the fire. Their brother, Ned, had a cottage nearby with some crab apples growing in the garden. There was much fun as he chased us away as we tried to grab a few.

All the people mentioned above have long passed away, God grant eternal rest to them all. They were at the heart of our rural community that lived in a warm and friendly place. There was no theft or robbery. We never locked the door of our house when we went to Mass on Sundays. One's bicycle was safe wherever you left it. I often hunted rabbits with a neighbouring pal, Joey Longworth, on Sunday evenings. We caught a few. They were good for the pot and if I sold one, I got three shillings and sixpence for it, a tidy sum for a young lad in those days. After hours of hunting and tea at Longworths, I would come home rather late at night, either round the road by Killare or on a moonlit night I would cross Roche's fields. Sometimes my parents would express concern that I was out so late but I never felt any danger. The countryside was totally safe. I left all this behind me in September 1944 to go away to St. Joseph's College Freshford, Co. Kilkenny.

Teresa and Chris in 1939

Teresa and Chris in Dublin 1948

Chapter Three
Going away to Boarding school

In early June, 1944, one Sunday morning in Boher after Mass, the parish priest, Fr. Mulvany, called me over and said to me, "Did you ever think of becoming a priest?" The question caught me by surprise. Many altar-boys see themselves standing at the altar if only as a passing thought. I had given it more serious consideration, even for a lad of thirteen and I simply said, "Yes, Father." He told me that there was a College in Kilkenny which accepted boys who were at least open to the idea of priesthood and he would write to the Rector on my behalf. I was delighted. I definitely had the priesthood in mind even at that early stage but whatever the future, the chance of a Secondary education was a real god-send. Secondary schooling in Ireland then was the privilege of the few. I wanted to continue schooling but where? Going to the local Diocesan College, St. Finian's in Mullingar, was beyond the family's financial resources. I had toyed with the idea of cycling to the Christian Brothers' school in Mullingar. Twelve miles each way daily might be alright in the summer but what about the winter months? So the opportunity of going to St. Joseph's College, Freshford, Co. Kilkenny, came as a great blessing.

Old Fr. Morris cycled up from Kilkenny – the war meant no private cars on the road because of petrol rationing – to interview my parents and I was enrolled to attend St. Joseph's the following September. It was a school run by the Mill Hill Missionaries, whose official name was St. Joseph's Society for Foreign Missions. Boys were accepted there for their secondary education provided they were at least open to the possibility of becoming missionary priests.

I got a list of the outfit necessary which I was glad to see included a pair of football boots. My sister, Teresa and myself, rode our bicycles into Athlone for a big day's shopping. The vast sum of twenty pounds covered most of the required items. We stopped in Moate on our way home for a cup of tea, feeling proud of our purchases. The days flew by as I prepared myself for boarding school at the beginning of September. My last day in Boher school was 21st July, 1944.

For someone who had never been to Dublin or even out of the county, the journey to Kilkenny was exciting. There was no direct connection by bus or train, so that meant an overnight stop in Dublin. Teresa, my big support during all this time, escorted me to Mullingar where we met a contingent of students mostly from the West, all heading for Kilkenny. It was led by Christy O'Connor from Longford, who was in his Leaving Cert. year. In the group there were half a dozen first year lads like myself and we made friends straight away. As we approached Dublin on the train from Mullingar we leaned out the window to get a good look at Croke Park well known to all of us from the radio broadcasts. That night we packed into a lodging house along the quays. I can still hear the clip-clop of the horses on the cobblestone street as they drew huge barges loaded with barrels of Guinness.

The next morning we got the train from Kingsbridge Station and two and a half hours later we arrived at Ballyragget where we all got off. Pat Rafter, a local man employed by the College was there with his big hay-cart. We loaded all our suitcases on to it. He set off for Freshford and we followed on foot, a journey of six miles. We reached the College in the afternoon. Later that evening a big contingent arrived from the South on the bus from Limerick. Thus began my 5 years at St. Joseph's College, Freshford. It was a small school, boarders only, with less than a hundred students. We were well treated. The food was good as the College had its own farm. Discipline was strict but unlike many other schools at the time there was no corporal punishment. All of our teachers were priests except for two laymen. They did their best and most of us came through the system with honours Inter and Leaving certificates. The years went by quickly. We were allowed home at Christmas and Summer, not at Easter. Football was the main outdoor sport and being reasonably good at it made it all the more pleasant for me.

1949, Chris with his parents along with Tom, Mary Jane and Mike.

Deciding the Future

During our years in the College we were encouraged to think about our future, to try to discern if we had a missionary vocation or not. We got talks from returning missionaries about life in Africa or Asia. Stories of missionary saints were read out during meals but by and large we had to make up our own minds. In my own case and I'm sure in the case of many others at that time, the dominant influences came from one's home. My own home was deeply Catholic, with Sunday Mass and nightly family Rosary, with pictures of the Sacred Heart and Our Lady prominently displayed. Neighbours would sometimes drop in for a chat in the evening and plenty of stories were told. Many of them concerned the fight for Irish freedom. The missionary magazines gave us tales of heroic missionaries in faraway places such as Africa and China. We all have high ideals when we are young. Springing from all this it seems that the two greatest ideals of the time were to live for God or to die for Ireland! During my Leaving Cert. Year I had no doubt that I wanted to be a missionary priest. Did my parents influence me unduly? No. I knew they would be proud to see me go on for the priesthood but always indicated it was entirely up to myself.

Studying for the Priesthood

In the autumn of 1949 six of the Leaving Class from Freshford went abroad to a Seminary in Rosendaal in the Netherlands to begin studies for the priesthood. There we would link up with students from Holland and Great Britain. Since Mill Hill was an International Missionary Society, it was planned that students from different countries should study for the priesthood together as after ordination we would be working together in far flung missionary countries. St. Joseph's Society was founded by Fr. Herbert Vaughan in 1866. He belonged to one of the old English Catholic families that managed to preserve their Catholic faith and some of their property despite years of persecution. His vision was to send missionaries wherever the British Empire was established to bring the Gospel of Christ to those peoples and to help them in every possible way. His future mission fields would include East and West Africa, India, Borneo and Malaysia. He bought a house in a north London district called Mill Hill as his first headquarters, so the Society, officially named St. Joseph's Society for Foreign Missions, later became known as the Mill Hill Missionaries. In 1866 Fr. Vaughan began with one priest (himself) and one student. He later became Bishop of Salford (Manchester) and ended up as Cardinal Archbishop of Westminster. He died in 1903 having seen much of his work come to great fruition. When the Society celebrated its centenary in 1966, it had already given over a thousand priests to the missionary apostolate.

St. Josef's Missiehuis, Rosendaal, provided a two year philosophy course in preparation for the priesthood. For us Irish students the journey there was long and tiresome. It was my first journey by boat. We travelled from Dun Laoghaire to Hollyhead on a small ferry called the Princess Maud, which had cramped conditions. The heavy rolling of the boat led to inevitable sea-sickness. There was the long journey by train to London. That night we took the train to Harwich to catch the boat to Hook van Holland. Then followed another long train journey to Rosendaal, via Rotterdam, in the south of Holland. The country was just recovering from the devastating effects of the German occupation. Rotterdam was still a bombed out city. Trains had just wooden seats. For us Irish it was the first glimpse of what war does to a country. We eventually reached the Missiehuis, the College where we would spend the next two years. There were about eighty students in all with slightly over forty in first year. Conditions were spartan. Heating was minimal. In winter I often had the break the ice on my washbasin before my morning ablutions. Now try shaving in those conditions! Our studies included philosophy, Sacred Scripture, and Church History. We got a smattering of Dutch which enabled us to communicate haltingly when we went out shopping in the local town. Visits out were strictly limited. We had six travel days in the year when we could travel afield, perhaps to Rotterdam or to Antwerp across the Belgium border. It took a while to adjust to the new studies especially philosophy. Football (soccer) was a good outlet for our youthful energies. The hardest thing of all was not being allowed home at Christmas.

All forms of tobacco were very cheap in Holland then, cigarettes, cigars, pipe tobacco and loose cigarette tobacco so that many rolled their own cigarettes. Smoking was almost a rite of passage into adulthood. Not to smoke was the exception. I bought into the lot, a pipe, boxes of cigars and cigarettes. During the recreation hour in the evening in the smoke-room, one could almost cut the air the smoke was so dense. The next morning the smell of stale tobacco was nauseous. Looking back now it seems all so foolish but we knew nothing then of the dangers of smoking. On returning to Ireland after the first year, I took six boxes of cigars home to Dad. I had remembered that during the war he enjoyed the occasional Havana cigar which my step-brother, Owen, would send him from New York wrapped up in a newspaper. However, Dad had little taste for the Dutch cigars but they became very popular with all the neighbours who would call in at night and light up in our kitchen much to the dismay of my mother. When I was going back to Holland for my second year, she begged me not to take any more cigars home. I duly obeyed her and by then I had given up smoking myself mostly because it affected my training for sports.

The two years in Holland passed quickly enough. We were encouraged to continue our discernment as regards continuing for the priesthood. Some of us found the going tough enough. The food was not great. Horse meat was sometimes part of the menu. The discipline was strict which I didn't mind but part of it was childish and totally unsuitable if we were meant to grow into mature adults. Half-way through first year I got totally fed-up and decided to leave. One evening I went up to the Rector to tell him of my decision. Strangely enough for someone who always told us the door was open if we wanted to leave, he spent the best part of an hour persuading me to change my mind. He did ask me if I had prayed much about my decision. That reminded me of a resolution I had once made during a retreat when I decided to go on for the priesthood, that if I ever changed my mind I would do so only after spending an hour in prayer before the Blessed Sacrament. That I had not done so I proceeded to the College Chapel determined to spend the hour and then leave! I can't say I got any great illumination during that hour but there was a dawning realisation that perhaps I was asking myself the wrong question, namely, do I want to be a priest or not, a reasonable question as after all it was my life to live. Yet when I asked another question, what does God want me to do with my life, I got the rather uneasy feeling that He wanted me to become a priest and I shouldn't run away from the challenge. So I decided to stay and continue. As a priest later on in many a retreat to various groups I often emphasised that the bottom line of all prayer is: God's will be done, not mine. Listening to God is often difficult especially if we are afraid He will ask us to face up to a difficult decision. We may try to run away but as Francis Thompson reminds us in *The Hound of Heaven*, the Lord will pursue us and guide us if we only listen.

I fled Him, down the nights and down the days;
I fled Him, down the arches of the years;
I fled Him, down the labyrinthine ways
Of my own mind, and in the midst of tears
I fled from Him.

Chapter Four:
St. Joseph's College, Mill Hill, London, Ordination

After two years in Holland, in September 1951, about thirty of us proceeded to St. Joseph's College in north-west London for our final four years of preparation for the missionary priesthood. Some students had left during our time in Holland. In Mill Hill, we were joined by three students from the Tyrol. Between the four classes in the Seminary there were over a hundred and twenty students. We first year students looked up to the top class who were Deacons preparing for their priestly ordination the following July. Our studies now included dogmatic and moral theology, sacred scripture, canon law and liturgy with a few lectures on mission theology. We saw our spiritual director individually once a month. This was to help us discern whether our vocation to the missionary priesthood was genuine or not. Towards the end of our first year we were invited to take a temporary oath committing ourselves to the Society for two years. A few of our class left at this stage, having decided that the priesthood was not for them

There was a regular routine of early rising, morning prayer and Mass. After breakfast we had to do some manual labour, such as sweeping corridors, preparing the lecture rooms and cleaning toilets. Then followed a programme of lectures and study. We had some free time. Discipline was strict. No radios or even novels in our rooms. We did have access to the radio and the daily papers in the common room which we could visit during our free time. Otherwise it was strictly off limits. I sometimes risked a violation of the rule. I can well remember coming down a darkened stairs late one Sunday evening to slip into the room where the radio was kept and listen quietly to the GAA results read out by Sean Og O'Ceallachain. That night in the Autumn of '53, I was delighted to hear that Boher had won the Westmeath Junior County championship. I had played for them all summer but had to return to College before the final.

At that time conditions in Britain had improved after the war. There was no more rationing of foodstuffs. Life in the Seminary was pleasant enough. Soccer was the main sports-game played. We had certain London days when we were free to visit the city and see the many tourist attractions. The British Museum, The Tower, Buckingham Palace, Madame Tussaud, Hyde Park and Windsor Castle were the usual targets. The great city of London has endless places of interest. Any of us keen on sports would try to fit in a good soccer game on a Saturday afternoon and I saw most of the top English clubs in action. We also managed to see some internationals games at Wembley stadium.

The four years slipped by quickly. Towards the end of our 3rd year we had to make a final decision. This was when we had to take an oath to serve the missionary Church in St. Joseph's Society for the rest of our lives. Academically we had to pass all sorts of exams. Morally, spiritually, character-wise, we had to pass the strict scrutiny of the staff. Some students might be advised to leave at this stage. It could be a tense enough time for some. Eventually 25 of our class made that final commitment. That meant we would go on to the final year, to be ordained Deacons after the Summer holidays and proceed to priestly ordination on the 2nd Sunday of the following July. For us that meant 10th July, 1955.

Were we well prepared for the big day of Ordination? Within the traditional system obtaining in Seminaries at that time, yes, we were reasonably well prepared. In hindsight one could point to many deficiencies in the system. There was little encouragement for creative thinking. Exam results were judged on one's ability to rehash the official text book. Moral questions were teased out ad nauseam stressing multiple prohibitions and obligations. Occasions of mortal and venial sins were multiplied indefinitely. I'm sure our moral theologians meant well but often the Good News of he Gospel was lost in a deluge of commandments and prohibitions.

There was also a lack of balance in presenting what constituted a grave sin. To eat meat on a Friday at the time when that was forbidden was classed as a grave sin. How can you compare that with serious violations of the moral law such as murder, adultery, widespread corruption, criminal violence or perjury?

Our formation for a life of celibacy was almost non-existent. We were warned to just keep away from any close contact with girls and to say our prayers! There were no lectures or discussions on meaningful relationships with women. We accepted our commitments and most of us felt that celibacy was very appropriate for the missionary priest. We also had the example of many of our immediate predecessors now on the missions, doing great work and coping with all sorts of situations. Apart from getting a few lectures from returning missionaries, we had little understanding of what lay ahead of us. Of course all this has changed in recent times.

Ordination

On 10th July 1955, twenty five of us were ordained in the small College chapel of St. Joseph's, Mill Hill. Because of the number, space was strictly limited and we were allowed just four visitors each. Sr. Catherine, Tom and Teresa and Mrs Maguire (a cousin) were my visitors. My Dad was now almost 97 years of age. My mother who had suffered badly from a leg injury was in poor health. It would have been wonderful to have them both present but the big celebration was reserved for the first Mass in St. Brigid's church, Boher, on 13th July when they and all the family, friends and parishioners could be present. Was my ordination day the happiest day of my life? Not really. I think I was too preoccupied with many things and at the time I was inclined to worry a lot. Some might call it a bout of scruples.

We were ordained by Cardinal Griffin and then we had breakfast with our family members. One hour later we were all called to the office of the Superior General, Fr. Thomas McLoughlin, a dour Scotsman. In his hand were twenty five envelopes which contained our appointments. We had been together for six years. Now we were missionary priests being appointed to different countries all over the world. In the evening we knelt together around the altar for the last time. We prayed together and sang a hymn of thanksgiving, shook hands all round, knowing some of us would never meet again. I was appointed to the staff of St. Joseph's College, Freshford, where I had been a student. Though wishing to go to the missions, I was glad of this appointment for one reason. I would be near my parents for some years at least and I knew a mission appointment would come later.

After all these years of preparation, awaiting the big moment.

Chapter Five
First Mass and Life after Ordination

I said my first Mass in Boher on the 13th July, the Wednesday following my ordination. On the Monday, I packed up my few belongings in the College, said goodbye to the staff and student colleagues. That night we had the long tiring journey from London to Hollyhead, then on to Dun Laoghaire and we arrived in Dublin early on Tuesday morning. Then came the journey home and meeting my mother and father for the first time as priest. They met me at the door of the old farmhouse. What emotions gripped us all. What thoughts must have gone through their minds? Dad was now near 97 years of age. We just hugged and kissed and I gave them my priestly blessing. The first Mass the following day was a big occasion, a chance to meet so many I would have liked to have had at my Ordination. The Church was packed. I got through it all right and said a few appropriate words. Afterwards most of the congregation came up to the altar rails for an individual blessing, many of the girls and boys with whom I had gone to school. I felt a bit embarrassed being called Father. I knew it was out of respect for the priesthood but I felt much more at home when people used my first name. Down the years I never had much time for the external trappings of honour that went with the clerical state. The pedestal was definitely not for me. The following Sunday I was playing for Boher football team with some of the local lads in Cusack Park, Mullingar.

The reception after the first Mass was in the Lake County Hotel, Mullingar, a lovely occasion for family and friends. I was so happy my parents could be there as my mother had been quite ill prior to my ordination and Dad despite his age was still very mobile and active. I like to think he was the star of the show. I often point out with pretended hurt that he got more congratulations than I did! I was so proud that he lived to see this day and could enjoy it to the full. The rest of the family, including my step-brother, Alexander, were all there except for my brother, Michael who was in New York. He had married the year before, had just bought a house and was unable to make the journey. He sent me a nice gift with a promise that if I got the opportunity to visit him, he would gladly pay my fare.

With my Parents after my first Mass in Boher 1955.
Dad was in his 97th year

That summer before I took up my first appointment in Freshford went by quickly. I had the privilege of saying Mass at home if I wished and did so often for the sake of my parents. I borrowed a car from a good neighbour and took my parents out for many a drive and visited relatives and friends. In doing so I was repaying Dad for the many times he took me out when I was just a nipper. On one occasion when we visited Dad's brother, my uncle Peter in Churchtown, my mother did not come along as she had a slight cold. Peter was a great talkative host. Neighbours would come in and the conversations ranged from the current political situation in Ireland to memories of travel in four different continents. Quite early on this particular evening, Dad turned to me and said, "Let's go home". I was surprised as he usually enjoyed a late night. "Fine, Dad, if you wish", I said. On the way home I asked him why the hurry and he turned to me as said, "I'm a bit worried about your mother". I'm afraid I dismissed his concern and said, "Dad, she's fine, just a bit of a cold." But Dad was anxious to get home as soon as possible. Driving into the yard of the old farmhouse, I had hardly time to open the door when Dad hopped out. My mother came to the porch and said, "You're home early". Dad, all of 97 years, clasped her in his arms, planted a big kiss on her lips and said, "Oh, Mary, I missed you all day"! Had I been a poet or an artist, how I would have loved to capture that scene for posterity, in words or on canvas. There is no generation gap where genuine love is concerned.

The Summer passed and soon it was time to report for the opening of the school term in early September in St. Joseph's College, Freshford, the very school where I had done my own secondary studies. My close friend and colleague who was ordained with me, Fr. Joe Jones, was also on the staff, as were others I knew quite well. In addition to teaching, I was put in charge of sports and various other activities, so life was busy and interesting. St. Joseph's was a small well run boarding school of less than a hundred students.

We participated in inter-college sports at football and basketball but with a limited pool to pick from, success was difficult. However, we had one great victory. Early in 1958 I spotted five students with overall sporting ability, mostly displayed in Gaelic football. I took them aside with a couple of others and three times a day we practised basketball. We entered the Senior Leinster Cup and in the early rounds got a fairly easy draw. We made the semi-finals. Both semi-finals and the final were due to be played in the Cahal Brugha Barracks, Dublin, together with the army final. We won our semi-final and then I took the players aside to watch the other semi-final. The team from St. Paul's, College, Raheny were hot favourites and rightly so. They were the reigning champions; they had four Irish youth internationals and they were coached by an expert from the American embassy. As we watched the semi-final which they won easily we could admire their versatility and technique. In an intense pre-match pep talk, I insisted that we could still beat them if we played to our strength. We were fitter than they were, so we must keep the game at a hectic pace. Don't let them slow it down as they were wont to do. We had the element of surprise. They expected a very easy game from an unknown team from the sticks! Because of their easy wins their tactics were predictable. We practised a method by which we could beat their zone defence.

The game started. Our plan worked like a dream. We were six points up before they knew what hit them. Then they called a time-out, now knowing that they had a tough game ahead. They changed tactics and tightened their defence. But we stuck to our plan, hustled them at every opportunity and swung the ball around. It became a war of attrition. Gradually they got our measure and they were a top class team. Still we kept ahead. We were four points ahead at half-time, two points ahead with a minute to go and then they drew level. Knowing they would have our measure in extra time, I called time-out and set up one last play. It worked. Don O'Connor sank a long one from far out and we were ahead again. They called a time-out. The whole place was in an uproar. All the

Dublin crowd that were not from St. Paul's wanted this unknown team to win. Even the time-keeper, a priest from Belcamp College, rushed from his chair to our huddle. He whispered hoarsely: "There's only 30 seconds left; for God's sake, hold them". There was still time for one more attack on our basket. It failed and we prevailed and were crowned Leinster Senior Basketball champions. I felt so proud of those five students who played their hearts out and proved the value of determination and guts, even when faced with superior opposition. Don O'Connor, Martin Gunning, Dan O'Connell, Paddy O'Connell and Eddie Prendergast were the heroes of the day.

Chapter Six
My years in St. Joseph's College
and Farewell to Dad

My years of teaching soon passed. I enjoyed the work and I had the benefit of long Summer holidays to spend with my parents as well as helping in the local parish. An important and pleasing aspect of each summer was my involvement with the Boher football team.

The Boher Team of 1957

Back Row, left to right: Paddy Conlon, Seamus Downes, Seamus McLoughlin, Michael Rabbitte, Vincent McCormack, Fr. Christy Fox, Michael McCormack, Fr. John Kerrane, Bill Carty, Gin Lynam, Jim Molloy, Paddy Meehan, Bill Kelly and Matt Casey.
Front Row: Eddie Rabbitte, Des Garland, Sean Stokes, Peter Stokes, Seamus Stokes, Paddy McLoughlin, J.J. Sheerin and Jack Duffy.

I was a member from the beginning and played for them all during my student days. As I studied abroad, I was usually gone back to College whenever they reached the final stages of the competition. So I missed the final in 1953 when they won the Championship. I continued playing after ordination when we won the Intermediate title and were promoted to senior ranks. We had a good team then and challenged the best. I usually played centre half back. We had some great games with Athlone, then Senior champions. In 1957, they just scraped past us by two points in Moate before going on to win the final. I have happy memories of all my team mates. They were a wonderful bunch of lads.

It was great to be with my family and help out on the farm during the summer. My mother's health was not too good due to an old leg wound which she partly neglected in the beginning. It became infected and developed into an ugly ulcer. She bore that cross with great courage and patience. In 1956 rural electrification was introduced across the country so the old homestead could now have decent lighting and some cooking and washing facilities which eased the burden of house keeping.

I bought a record player and some long playing records as Dad enjoyed listening to the old Irish ballads.

When I came home for Christmas 1957 I was amazed to see that Dad still liked to stroll around the farmyard. He was now in his hundredth year. I was afraid he might slip and fall outside. He loved his walk even when the weather was cold. One showery day I found he had gone out and I chased after him with umbrella and overcoat. "Dad, you'll catch your death of cold". He smiled and said "Sure it's only a little squall". We sat in an old shelter and he told me stories of Argentina long ago.

The March of 1958 was a particularly cold month. Dad would be 100 in September. We were already thinking of a celebration to mark the occasion but it was not to be. On 25th March, Dad was up and about as usual but he had a certain premonition and told my mother he would like to see a priest. She asked him if she should send for their son, Fr. Christy. My father replied, "I don't care whose son he is as long as he's a priest." Fr. Mulvany who attended him regularly came in the afternoon and Dad received the last rites of the Church. Afterwards he was up and about as usual. Some neighbours called in that evening. Dad retired after the Rosary but his final remark to my brother Tom was how happy he was that night.

The following morning Mum brought him a cup of tea which he tasted. He asked what day it was. Mum told him it was the 26th March, the birthday of their second daughter, Mary Jane. He looked at the picture of the Blessed Mother over the bed and gave a sigh of thanksgiving. His head slipped sideways and he passed away without another word. Of course, we were sorry he didn't make the hundred but I wouldn't have changed that ending for any amount of extra years.

Dad was 'waked' in the house in the traditional Irish fashion which is considered a most wholesome way of meeting the mystery and sorrow of death. The deceased was laid out in the bedroom. Neighbours came in during the day and throughout the night to offer their sympathies. The custom was to sprinkle the corpse with holy water and say a prayer for the departed. The Rosary was said. There were plenty of refreshments available, tea and coffee and stronger stuff! Stories were told recalling the life of the deceased, always complimentary and often humorous. The family welcomed the great support. The body was 'coffined' and taken to the church the following day where it remained overnight.

I said the Requiem Mass the following morning. I felt so sad saying farewell to such a beloved father. The Mass included prayers of thanksgiving for a long and fruitful life now gathered to the Lord. The funeral was in the afternoon. The procession took place from the church to the graveyard nearby where we said the final prayers. Dad's eldest son, Owen, flew into Shannon from New York that morning. He had not arrived so I delayed a little. I was about to conclude when the taxi arrived. Owen rushed over afraid that he would be too late. He made a request. Would it be possible to see his father? I felt why not. The lid of the coffin was removed. Owen knelt and kissed Dad, sprinkled holy water and said a prayer. Then we replaced the lid, concluded the ceremony and Dad was laid to rest beside his parents. Years later Owen told me how grateful he was for being allowed that simple gesture.

I was often asked the secret of Dad's longevity. Undoubtedly his strong constitution, his relaxed life-style, his balanced simple diet, all played their part. He smoked his pipe and enjoyed an occasional pint of Guinness. I'm convinced that the greatest factor was his integrity and his wholesome outlook on life. He faced his many problems with great serenity. "Ah sure, it could be worse!" he would often say. He was generous to a fault. After his death, some neighbours came to tell me how he helped them in their difficulties, some financial. This touched me very much because as a family we too were struggling to make ends meet. Dad had a helping hand and a kind word for everybody. His death marked the end of an era.

Visits to New York

Twice during my time in Freshford I spent two summers in New York. I made my first trip in June 1958 with two priest colleagues. We flew out from Shannon at midnight on Pan Am. There were no Aer Lingus transatlantic flights then. In those pre-jet days it was a thirteen hour flight direct to N.Y. It was my first time to fly and I enjoyed it. In the fifties visiting the U.S. was a big deal. I vividly remember flying in over Long Island in the early morning hours and gazing out the window to catch sight of the great country we had heard so much about.

Mike and Owen met me at Idlewild airport (not yet JFK). They had a great welcome for me. At the airport then there was a balcony overlooking customs. I looked up and saw both my brothers looking down on me and waving, the first time I saw them since the summer of '49. That year Owen visited Ireland. It was then that he suggested to Mike that he should come to America as job opportunities were few in Ireland. What a reunion we had. Our first port of call was Owen's parish church where he had arranged for me to offer Mass and then back to his house in the Bronx where Bridie, Owen's wife, had prepared a great meal for all of us. Later on Mike ordered a taxi to take us both to his house in Queen's where his wife Peggy had a great welcome and introduced me to their two little daughters, Mary and Margie. Later in the evening Mike took me shopping to purchase two light black suits suitable for the New York Summer. I was beginning to get my first taste of the humid, stifling NY summer weather for which my heavy black suit was totally unsuitable.

After a pleasant few days we had to report to our Society house in upstate NY near Albany. There we were assigned to some parishes to help the local priests. I spent a few weeks in St. Peter's in Schnectedy. During that time Alan Clancy, an important figure in G.A.A. circles in New York, invited me up to play for Monaghan in Gaelic Park, one Sunday, which I did. We won the match but I was completely out of practice and prudently declined further invitations. My brother, Mike, lent me his car. I had first to do a driving test to get a N.Y. driving license as my Irish license was not recognised. No wonder. In those days in Ireland one got a driving license from the P.O. on just paying the license fee. With Mike's car I had the freedom of the roads and my parish assignments allowed me considerable latitude. Upstate New York is beautiful countryside and I was able to take trips into the Catskill mountains and even travel as far as Niagara Falls. For me it was a wonderful summer.

I returned to the States in the Summer of '61, again to help out in parishes and to spend some time with family and friends. I will remember that summer for one significant reason. In mid-July I was based in a parish in Rhode Island and one morning I casually picked up my post, surprised to see a letter to me from the Superior General in Mill Hill, London. It read:

"Dear Fr. Fox, my Council and I have decided to appoint you to the diocese of Tororo in Uganda. We expect you to report to the Bishop there and take up your appointment by November of this year. We thank you for your service in Freshford and wish you every blessing and success in your future missionary work.

Yours Sincerely,

Thomas McLoughlin."

It was a total surprise. At that time there were no consultations beforehand as regards appointments. You just went where you were told to go. I had to look up the map to find out where Tororo was. Mission assignments were for eight years. The family both in Ireland and in the States were surprised too. They were accustomed to my being around. Saying goodbye to them all was very painful, especially giving my mother a farewell hug wondering if I would ever see her again as her health was rather poor. In hindsight, it was a timely appointment. I had been ordained six years. I was a missionary priest, so it was time to set foot on real mission territory and I had always felt I would end up in Africa.

Chapter Seven
Uganda, here I come

On a blustery November day in 1961 we set sail from Tilbury Docks in London on board the 'Warwick Castle'. It was a small ship, part of the Union Castle line. There were a few hundred passengers on board, many returning to Kenya and South Africa after visiting the U.K. There were eight Mill Hill Missionaries aboard including five Irishmen, Fr. Bart Hayes from Kerry, Fr. Kevin O'Rourke from Leitrim, two newly ordained priests, Fr. Bob Staunton from Cork and Fr. Terry Gogarty from Naas, Co. Kildare and myself. We were appointed to work in different dioceses in Kenya and Uganda. Our voyage took us round Gibraltar, through the Mediterranean Sea, along the coast of Italy, through the Suez canal, down the Indian Ocean to Mombasa on the east coast of Kenya. There we were due to disembark.

There were plenty of stops on the way and I thoroughly enjoyed the journey. We put into Genoa for three days which enabled us to get a night train to Rome, have a hectic sight-seeing day in that great city and return in time to continue the on-going voyage. At Port Said we were given the opportunity of a day trip to Cairo and join the boat again at the other end of the Suez canal. The trip to Cairo included a visit to the Museum to view the magnificent treasures of Tutankhamun's tomb. It also included a visit to the pyramids and a ride on a camel to view them on the outside.

I picked the biggest camel I could find which seemed to have the biggest and roughest looking driver as well. When I was being taken to the other side of an outlying pyramid with cries of "Hi, Ho, Silver", I thought I was being offered a special treat. Then suddenly

I realised we were alone, away from all the others. The camel driver jerked the reins out of my hands and demanded money, all I had. I was taken completely aback. Yet even when he threatened, "Money or I kill you", I had time to size up the situation. Having survived the rough and tumble of Gaelic football, the son of Mike Fox, ex-Argentina, even though he had no pipe to wave as an imitation gun, was not going to be intimidated by a grizzly old man. From my lofty perch on the camel I leaned down and shook my fist in his face and swore something at him by the Tomb of Tutankhanum! Without warning he gave the camel a sharp jab under the withers and the animal took off like a guided missile across the Sahara with me hanging on to the hump for dear life. Even then I reckoned the animal would soon get tired and the driver would eventually have to recall him, which he did. The walk back to base was a rather silent pilgrimage. When I got off I produced the voucher/payment ticket. He reached out his hand. I dropped the ticket on the ground. As he picked it up. I put a finger in his face and warned him, "Don't ever try that again!" On the return bus journey to the boat a lady passenger told me she had a similar experience and gave whatever money she had to the driver. Fortunately she did not carry much.

We boarded the ship again at port Suez and sailed down the Red Sea. Our next call was Aden. Part of the fun of these short port stops was haggling with the many peddlers who came alongside the boat with their wares. There were plenty of good bargains to be got, binoculars, cameras, leather bags and a whole range of colourful clothing but one had to be shrewd as there were plenty of fakes as well.

On we sailed south along the African coast. There was a great ceremony when we crossed the equator, songs and laughter and a few comely maidens being dumped into the swimming pool. There were plenty of deck games so plenty of fun and entertainment. I teamed up with a gorgeous South African girl to win the deck-quoits mixed doubles. She was an average player but in her trendy outfit she was a great distraction to the opposition!

Eventually we reached Mombasa, our port of disembarkation. I thought of the first band of Mill Hill Missionaries, a Bishop and three priests, who arrived here in April of 1895. The area assigned to them for their apostolate stretched roughly from what is now Kampala, capital of Uganda, to deep into Kenya, an area bigger than Ireland. They had to walk from the coast and had to organise their daily trek with provisions for each day. They followed an old trail into the interior made by early traders. They had many instructions about protecting themselves from the tropical sun. The routine was to pitch tent at mid-day before the sun got too hot and strike camp each morning at about four o'clock. They reached Kampala in September after several months of rough travel.

They started work immediately, establishing small mission centres. Other bands of missionaries followed. The third caravan in 1903 had the advantage of railway travel as far as Nairobi. The great East African Railway was under construction at the time. It would eventually reach Kisumu and Kanpala. Over sixty years later, we could build on the work of those great pioneers. In the area where they had sown the first seeds, there were now several well established dioceses with churches, schools and hospitals. Together with a colleague, Fr. Bob Staunton, I was appointed to the diocese of Tororo, Uganda. We arrived at the local railway station in at 2.30 one morning after a thirty-six hour train journey from Mombasa. A colleague met us with a minivan and took us to St. Peter's College, Tororo, where we spent the next few days meeting colleagues and getting used to our new surroundings before heading to our assigned parishes. I was appointed to Madera parish near Soroti in the north and Fr. Bob to Usuk parish still further north. We met the Bishop and the Society Superior who gave us plenty of advice as seasoned missionaries were wont to do and wished us well. A few days later we headed north and began our missionary apostolate.

I enjoyed the work from the start. St. Patrick's parish, Madera was a huge parish by Irish standards with some twenty outstations. The parish priest was Fr. Eef van Rassel, a hard-working Dutchman.

After the initial rough edges were smoothed over on both sides we got on well together. My first task was to learn the local language, in this case Teso, one of the more difficult languages in Uganda where there are some seventeen different tribal languages. I'm not over gifted in languages but did make some progress and within a few weeks was given faculties to hear confessions and minister the sacraments in the vernacular. Parish work consisted mainly of pastoral activities, saying Mass, hearing confessions, visiting schools and baptising infants. There was usually a sizeable number of adults receiving instruction in the Catholic faith in preparation for baptism. There were many sick people to be visited. Most parishes had a supply of medicines for the benefit of these people. I went regularly to one of the outstations and often stayed a few days there visiting the people and helping them in whatever way I could. The local catechist took me around to visit those who needed me. He usually provided the basic food, which often consisted of boiled chicken and matoke (local plantain). At night I sometimes slept under the stars.

Missionaries are sometimes accused of proselytising and imposing their own western values on age-old cultures, a form of neo-colonialism. We are asked: why go to Africa in the first place? I make no apology for the missionary apostolate of bringing the message of Christ to others as Our Saviour commanded us to do. Of course there is a danger for us of presenting the Good News of the Gospel with certain western trappings. We must guard against this and missionaries were often the first to study the local culture and to affirm all that is good in it. Every culture has to be examined in the light of the teaching of Christ, our own western culture included. Some of our missionaries were pioneers in studying the local language and putting it into print form with grammar and dictionary.

There can be serious challenges for the missionary, for instance how to deal with the widespread practice of polygamy in parts of Africa. If a husband dies leaving wife and children, his brother, even though married, will inherit the wife and family. It is a form of social protection. So what has the Church to say to that?

Africans have a deep belief in a spirit world, the spirits of ancestors and other unknown forces. This can give rise to various forms of superstition and we have to learn how to cope with them. Let me give one simple example. A woman once came to me in fear of death claiming someone had put an evil spell on her and she was going to die. She was genuinely terrified. Rational argument is no use in such a case. Knowing something of local beliefs, I simply told her that she was lucky to come to me as my prayers were more powerful than the spell of any witchdoctor. I prayed at length for the healing power of Jesus in her life, blest her and told her to return to me for two more sessions. As she had confidence in me she was freed from her awful dread and recovered.

Another case had a sad ending. A boy in our Junior Seminary developed cancer in his knee and the doctor recommended amputation. His mother refused to allow it. She wanted to find out the reason for the cancer and took him home. She called in the local witchdoctor. He demanded a goat, killed it, poured some blood around and after much mumbo-jumbo informed the woman that the boy had stepped on an evil spirit and this was the spirit's revenge. Such nonsense! After visiting the boy twice and seeing his growing weakness, I'm afraid I lost my temper and told the woman in no uncertain terms that she was the one responsible for her son's death. The following morning she arrived at the school in a taxi with her son, transferred him to the back of my car and went away without a word. When I came out of the classroom I discovered the boy who told me to do whatever I wanted. I rushed him to the hospital. The operation seemed successful. He was measured for an artificial leg but then sadly secondaries set in and he died within a few weeks. If prompt action had been taken he could have been saved.

To work effectively with people there is the need to study deeply all aspects of their culture, their understanding of marriage and family life, community, work and leisure, death and the after life. It is a life-long study. Fatalism plays a big part in the lives of many people and I will refer to this again when I write about the fight against the spread of AIDS.

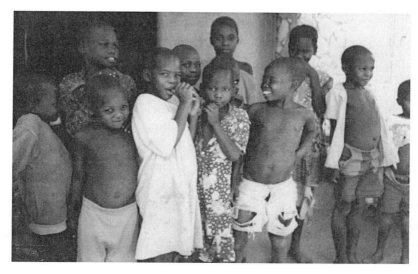

Now who is that tall new missionary? Will he organise some football?

1961, First foray into Africa. Madera parish, Eastern Uganda.

Chapter Eight
Back to Teaching

By October 1962, I was settling in well to missionary work, getting to know the people, becoming more proficient at the local language and studying their culture. I was enjoying the work. The Catholic mission compound was always a great centre of activity. In Madera we had St. Patrick's church, a big primary school, a vocational school, a school for blind children run by the Sisters. Nearby was a big government secondary school for which we supplied a chaplain. In the area was a very successful Agricultural Institute at Arapai, established and run by Mel Arthurs from Northern Ireland. He and his wife, Rosaleen, and their growing family, became lifelong friends and we remained in close touch after he left and settled in Devon.

The town of Soroti, just a mile away, was bustling with activity. Most of the shops were run by Indians or Goans and were well stocked. There was a tennis club and a swimming pool. Truly in the early sixties in Uganda we had the best of both worlds. We were doing a good job helping the people not only spiritually but in a thousand different ways and there was a great sense of peace and security at the time. One could move freely even at night. At the mission house we often played bridge on Sunday evenings. Two priests from a neighbouring mission would join us for supper, evening prayer and then a long session of cards. There was a great spirit of camaraderie among missionaries. Overnight hospitality was easy to offer. All you needed was a mattress and clean sheets and a room free of cockroaches and mosquitoes. Mosquito spray was much in demand.

One of my colleagues, Fr. Franz Strater, from Holland, had a great interest in snakes. He kept about a dozen of them in various containers in his room and around his house, which was given a wide berth by most people especially the local Africans who have a horror of snakes. When Prince Bernhard of the Netherlands touched down at the local airstrip on his way to northern Uganda on a hunting safari, Fr. Strater felt he should be there to greet him and give him a little surprise! After the formal handshake Fr. Strater said, "I've something to show you" and suddenly pulled out a snake from a box and twirled it around. I don't think the prince was much amused, nor was his bodyguard!

Later in the year Fr. Strater was due to go on leave. He asked me to take him to Entebbe airport. What I didn't know and what nobody else knew was that one of his bags contained a live snake. Stories differ. He says he declared it and was told O.K. I doubt it. The fact is that the snake was put on board a KLM flight to Amsterdam in the luggage compartment. First stop was Rome. Passengers disembarked. There was a long delay. Suddenly a group of *carbinieri* was seen rushing through the airport and surrounding the plane. Shouts of 'un serpente enorme' were heard. Apparently the snake escaped during the flight and greeted one of the Italian bag handlers with a mighty hiss when he opened the luggage compartment. Fr. Strater, waiting with the others inside the airport, suspected something and rushed out, told the police that he could handle it. He climbed up among the luggage, spotted the tail of the snake sticking out from behind a big suitcase, found the bag, grabbed the snake, stuffed it into the bag and tied a firm knot on it He came down the steps, assured the panic-stricken guards that all was well and not to worry. As he re-entered the airport with the snake in the bag across his shoulders, the crowd gave a good imitation of the parting of the waves of the Red Sea when Moses appeared! Fr. Strater was staying in Rome for a few days. That evening officials of the KLM called to his hotel room and demanded to know what happened to the snake. He tried to bluff them saying that he had ended his journey. It was none of their business. When they threatened to get a search warrant he gave in and admitted the snake was in a bag in the wardrobe. They insisted that it be killed immediately and even threatened legal action. Fortunately for him a rumour had gone round that he was an eccentric friend of prince Bernhard and no further action was taken. When the KLM officials had gone, Fr. Stater dumped the dead snake in the wastepaper basket, called room service and asked a young attendant to empty the basket. The lad was half-way down the stairs when he saw what was in the basket. There was a scream. Fr. Strater looked out to see the basket and a bloody and very dead snake strewn down the stairs. He gathered the mess up, put it into a sack, went outside, took a bus till it crossed the Tiber. He went to the middle of the bridge and threw the whole lot into the river. End of the snake drama. He told me all about it when he came back from leave.

Back at the mission, the parish priest decided to take short break and left me in charge. I was very happy there and looked forward to doing my bit for the development of the parish. There was great need for more schools. With help from home I bought a plot and put up a simple structure. We started with a few tree trunks for benches. We got some basic equipment, employed a teacher and began. There was great pride in seeing that school develop and young people get a chance of an education they would not otherwise get. We provided some basic medicine to people who were badly in need of it. There were many child baptisms and also a group of adults receiving Christian instruction preparing for Baptism.

I looked forward to a full term of such pastoral work. It was not to be. At the diocesan junior seminary, a priest teacher had to go home for health reasons and they badly needed a replacement. As I had experience of teaching I got a letter from the Bishop one morning thanking me for my work at Madera and appointing me to teach at Nagongera Seminary. It was located in the south of the diocese near the town of Tororo. I was not too happy leaving Madera but I always trained myself to make the best of any situation. When the parish priest came back I said goodbye and reported for duty for my new assignment. I returned to St. Patrick's every Christmas and Easter to help out with the extra pastoral work.

It was easy to settle into the routine of teaching again. We had a good staff and African students were always keen to learn. I helped out with the sports programme and played soccer with the students. Most of them played in their bare feet which in no way inhibited their ball control and powerful shooting. We built up a good team and one year beat St. Peter's College, Tororo, home and away, much to their dismay as they were a much bigger school than ours.

As this was to be my home for the next five years, I joined the Tororo club which had a tennis court, swimming pool and a nine hole golf course. I got myself an old set of Fred Daly golf clubs and enjoyed a weekly game of golf. There were still many Europeans in the area, some teachers and many working in the local cement factory. Uganda was a Protectorate, not a colony so no colonial settlers. Most overseas personnel were civil servants, teachers or administrators. There was a healthy friendly relationship with the local people. Besides, I always felt that Ugandans in general were the warmest, friendliest people one could meet.

Uganda became an independent Republic within the Commonwealth on 9th October, 1962. It made little difference to us at the time. Not many Europeans left and life continued as usual. Some teachers from overseas were recruited to teach at secondary level. There were four of them attached to St. Peter's College, Tororo. John Hughes from Scotland was head of the English department. His house became a meeting place for many of us. After a game of golf, a long cool beer tasted great, as we sat outside in the tropical evening exchanging many stories. John had been in the RAF during the war, was shot down over Germany, recovered from his wounds and in addition to teaching, became an accomplished boxer and coach. He introduced boxing into Uganda, coached their Olympic squad and was with them at the Rome Olympics. He and his wife Joyce and their growing family became my lifelong friends.

As a teacher I always took pride in the success of the students. Some of them are now priests in the local diocese and one later became a bishop. As I was in Uganda at the time I had the honour of presenting him for Episcopal ordination.

Teaching also allowed for a fairly regular lifestyle. We could use the school holidays to pursue our own interests. I travelled a lot, getting to know the country better. On a couple of occasions, Fr. Bill McAvoy, a priest colleague and I visited some game parks. In those days, before the country was torn apart by the rise of Idi Amin, Uganda had many tourists. The Queen Elizabeth game park and the Kabarega national park, with its spectacular Murchison Falls, were unrivalled for scenery and for viewing game. There were great herds of elephants, buffaloes, wildebeest and a huge variety of antelope. One could almost walk across the Nile river on the backs of hippos they were so plentiful but not to be recommended! There were crocodiles by the dozen in the water with many basking on the river bank. From the security of the boat, I once threw a sizeable piece of log into an open mouth and got a demonstration of the power of those crushing jaws.

Fr. Eddie Bennet, another colleague, had two brothers working commercially in Tanzania. Both were married and had houses near Arusha. We spent some vacation time with them and enjoyed some tennis, golf and touring. With a borrowed land –rover we toured the Lake Manyara region. The famous Ngorongoro crater is nearby. We descended the narrow steep road to the bottom. The huge stretch of land measuring several miles across is undoubtedly the greatest sanctuary of wild-life in Africa. The key rule on these occasions is to stay within the vehicle. Two lions strolled up to the vehicle and literally looked in the widow. One rhino considered we had come too close. He charged us as we drove away and gave our vehicle a solid bump with his horn. There were vast herds of elephants, wildebeest, zebra and antelope.

A well-known Irishman lived in the area where he ran a big coffee estate. He was Bob Tisdale who had won a gold medal for

Ireland in the 1932 Los Angeles Olympics in the four hundred metres hurdles. He was happy to talk to anyone like myself with a keen interest in sports. We often talked long into the night. He told me that the afternoon he won his medal was a great day for Ireland as Dr.Pat O'Callaghan won a gold medal for the hammer throw on the same day. These were the days of the purely amateur sports. When a reporter asked Bob the secret of his success, he answered "A pint of Guinness a day!". Later Bob retired to Australia and I read that at the time of the Sydney Olympics in 2000 he was the oldest living Olympic champion and was invited to present the medals to the winners of the four hundred metres hurdles, an invitation which he declined.

Mt. Kilimanjaro

Touring Tanzania one was always conscious to the majestic, towering presence of Mt. Kilimanjaro. Its snow capped summit shone brightly in the tropical sunshine. The early Europeans couldn't understand how there could be snow on the equator. It must be salt, white rock or something else. To the local African population the snow capped peak symbolised the milk that would never dry up in their mothers' breasts. The mountain is the highest in Africa and it is claimed to be the single highest peak in the world, the others being part of a mountain range. It is nineteen thousand three hundred feet high. There are two peaks, Mawanzi at about seventeen thousand feet and Mt. Kibo. There is a stretch of saddle territory in between at about fifteen thousand feet. Mt. Kibo is in fact an extinct volcano. The summit is a huge snow covered rim surrounding a vast crater. It is a very distinctive feature of the border between Kenya and Tanzania. It is a spectacular sight even at night time when it can be seen shining by moonlight. To anyone who likes a challenge, it poses an invitation to climb.

So it was that on my next vacation from school in January 1964, Donald MacCullach, a teacher from Scotland, and myself prepared for the challenge. We set off for Moshi and put up at the Catholic mission there. Early next morning we were at the bottom of the mountain ready to go. There we met a small group of American students intent on the same. The ascent from the Tanzanian side requires no special equipment. One needs sturdy boots and one's whole body well padded, woolly scarf and balaclava, gloves and plenty of protective face cream. The only equipment we carried was a long solid walking stick. We hired a couple of porters and a guide. The latter was necessary to show us the proper safe route. There was snow from seventeen thousand feet. This covered many a dangerous crevasse into which one could easily slip. We had a primus stove and basic rations and off we set. It was highly recommended that we take three days at least for the climb. This was mainly to adjust to the altitude. The first day was a relatively easy uphill stroll to twelve thousand feet where we pitched camp, relaxed and partook of some refreshments.

It was relatively early in the afternoon. There was a forest belt of trees near us but we were advised not to venture too far in as there might be leopards or elephants around. I walked up a path for half a mile and sat on an old tree trunk to say a few prayers from my breviary. You couldn't image a more peaceful scene. Suddenly I got the fright of my life hearing quick sharp breathing right behind me. I thought of leopard, cheetah, whatever. No, it was human. A young American had become totally disorientated by the altitude, was rushing about and obviously did not know where he was. I hailed him and asked if he was OK. "Sure," he said, I'm about to climb that peak". "Which one?" I asked. "Mount McKinley" he shouted. I told him he was far from Alaska and took him by the arm and led him down the mountain to our camp where he recovered.

The second day was a steeper climb and we reached an old campsite at fifteen thousand feet. There we rested and prepared for the final climb to the summit of Mt. Kibo. The guide told us we would leave at two a.m., that it would be dark and that the ascent would take four hours. The aim was to be on the summit at dawn to watch the sun rise up in the east seeming to come up out of the Indian Ocean and bathe the whole of Africa in glorious light.

The time passed slowly. Some of us tried to sleep a bit on the hard ground. I went for a stroll across the saddle. It was so quiet and still I could imagine myself being on the face of the moon! We assembled at one o'clock. Someone made porridge and offered me a few spoonfuls, laced with brandy, all to strengthen one for the final ascent. The guide gave us strict instructions. The steep ascent would require a zig-zag approach; that we would walk for two minutes, then pause for thirty seconds, lean on our walking sticks, breathe deeply and then continue. We must keep to that routine and not look up. The guide walked ahead and called the shots. It worked well. At seventeen thousand feet the snow got deeper and covered much loose scree. It was a question of two steps forward and slide one back. Suddenly I felt violently sick and threw up everything. The guide who was paid by contract immediately suggested going back. It was just what I needed. I said "No way. Forward everybody" and fortunately I soon felt well again. The routine continued. I did chance a few glances upward and understood the psychology of not looking up. There was nothing but blackness ahead as if we had made no progress but we had and sure enough just before dawn we reached the rim of the crater. It is called Gilman's Point. I knew that a corresponding section of the rim on the other side of the crater, called "Uhuru Peak," was a couple of hundred feet higher. The guide who felt his work was done reluctantly took us along the rim to the other side, an exciting walk with glaciers stretching down on one side and deep caverns on the other. We soon reached Uhuru Peak. It was dawn and so we watched the sunrise. The air was crystal clear. Literally looking down on Africa from the top of its highest mountain, the views were spectacular. I took some slides, not sure if they would be all right as I was trying to balance my camera in my ungloved, freezing fingers. The slides came out fine, beautiful reminders of a never-to-be forgotten experience. Goggles were needed to protect the eyes from the blazing sunshine. One other little ritual we had to perform. Donald had taped a seven iron golf club to his walking stick and now produced some golf balls. We took turns at hitting them into the vast crater. Some photos were taken with the vain idea of flogging them to an advertising agent. "Yes, even on the top of Kilimanjaro, I still use Dunlop 65!" Ah, if only we were celebrities, we might have made some money! We remained on the summit for about four hours till the clouds started drifting in and we felt it was time to descend. We made the descent in one day and that evening I was happy to immerse myself in a warm hot bath at the mission station and soothe the blisters on my feet. The next day, Donald and I drove to Mombasa to relax and celebrate. Later it was good to report to the members of Tororo Club on our achievement and to collect a few modest bets from sceptics who claimed we would never manage to do the climb.

Chapter 9
End of my first Tour in Africa:
Home Leave

Our early missionaries were appointed to the foreign missions for life. When one considers the climate and conditions obtaining in some of the mission countries one can only admire their courage and dedication. Africa was called the white man's grave because of the prevalence of tropical diseases such as malaria, dysentery and sleeping sickness. Many of our early missionaries survived for only a few years.

Yet new volunteers continued to come. They established churches, schools, hospitals and social centres. In 1903, Bishop Hanlon persuaded a group of Religious Sisters from the Abbey in Mill Hill to come to Uganda to cater especially for women's healthcare and education. These Sisters did marvellous work in both areas. The youngest member of that first band of pioneer Sisters was Teresa Kearney from Co. Wicklow. She later became the leader of the group. She became famous as Mama Kevina and spent over fifty years of dedicated ministry in Uganda. Among her many achievements was the establishment of Nsambya Hospital in Kampala and also two leper hospitals to cater for victims of that dreaded disease which was rampant in some parts of Uganda at the time.

In 1957 the tour of duty for members of our Society was reduced to ten years, later on to eight and during my first tour in Uganda it was reduced to five. I looked forward to my first home leave in 1967. One of the hardest aspects of being a missionary abroad is missing out on family events, whether joyful or sad. During my first term in Uganda, my step-brother, Alexander, died. My brother, Tom, got married, and quite a few nephews and nieces were born. I kept in touch with home mostly by letters. The telephone system at the time was most unreliable. Although I enjoyed my work as a teacher and at the same time was much involved in retreat work, I looked forward to a vacation at home. When the time came near I felt a bit like a schoolboy going on vacation from boarding school for the first time.

Early in 1967 I said goodbye to all my friends in Uganda and headed for home. I was entitled to six months leave, a month for every year spent on the missions. I travelled Arab Airlines from Entebbe to Heathrow via Cairo. The airline allowed one to break the journey in Cairo with free detour to the Holy Land and back at no extra cost. I availed of this great opportunity and after a few days in Cairo, flew to Jerusalem. I spent a week there. Being on my own I could wonder around as I pleased. What a privilege to be able to visit so many places made sacred by the presence of Jesus. The Church of the Holy Sepulchre is built over what is reckoned to be the site of Calvary and the Sacred Tomb. I was able to say Mass there. What a privilege to be able to spend a quiet evening of reflection and prayer in the Garden of Gethsemani. I visited Bethlehem and said Mass where Jesus was born. I was truly overwhelmed by the whole experience.

On returning to Cairo I resumed my flight to Heathrow and then on to Dublin. My sister, Teresa, her husband Benny and some of their children were waiting for me at the airport. What a re-union, the hugs and the kisses and then off to their home in Navan where my mother was staying at the time. The old home near Killare was empty as Tom was still in America. My mother had been unwell before I left and I wondered if I would ever see her again. Now here she was to greet me, looking better than ever. Teresa's third son, young Bernard was very interested in the colourful African drum I had taken home. Early next morning he was really thumping it up and down on the road outside. This was something none of the other kids around ever had. Teresa's eldest son, Michael, was away in boarding school and the rest were at home, Aidan, Colin, Imelda and Sean, not yet a year old.

My next visit had to be to Newtown, Horseleap where my sister, Mary Jane and her husband, Michael Carton, lived. Again it was lovely to meet their growing family, Mary Frances, Bridget, Pat, Margaret and Catherine. One of the great blessings of my life as a celibate priest is the close relationships I always had with my brothers and sisters and a host of nephews and nieces, to say nothing of our far-flung family of cousins.

It took a little while to re-adjust to conditions back home after spending so long away. One had to get used to the Irish winter again after years of tropical sunshine. I was intrigued about how the weather provided such a topic of conversation when people meet. It is indeed a safe subject.

I offered to help out in St. Mary's, Navan, and was given a warm welcome by Fr. Joe Abbott and his colleagues. I've always liked to be involved in pastoral work as much of my life was involved with teaching. I was happy to help out with the Masses in St. Mary's and be available for confessions and other pastoral duties.

I planned my six months leave carefully. It entailed a thirty day Retreat in Rome beginning in February followed by a visit to New York after Easter. My step- brother, Owen and his wife Bridie, lived in the Bronx. Tom had married Delia Kelly the year before I came home and they now had a baby daughter, Mary. They lived in Queens and were preparing to return to Ireland to the home in Killeenbrack where a new house had been built. My other brother, Michael, also lived in Queens with his wife, Peggy, and their growing family, Mary, Margie, Mike Jn., Kathleen and Teresa. Their youngest son, Kevin, was not yet born. They too were thinking of returning to Ireland for good. For them it would be a huge decision. I really looked forward to meeting them all again.

The Retreat in Rome was at the Jesuit centre, Villa Caveletti, south of the city. It consisted of a month long programme of prayer, reflection and spiritual direction guided by a priest. Conferences are based on the spirituality of St. Ignatius of Loyola which sees God at the heart of all creation and gives clear guidance how to discern His will in all our decisions.

I celebrated Easter in Ireland with Teresa and her family. In May I booked my trip to the United States for what I thought would be a pleasant time before heading back to Uganda or so I thought.

Chapter 10
A new Appointment

I travelled to New York in May 1967. Three of my brothers now lived there with their families and it was great to meet up again and hear their stories while they in turn wanted to know about my work in Africa. I was meeting Tom's wife, Delia, for the first time and their baby daughter, Mary. There were plenty of cousins around too and we had some great reunions. The New York Westmeath Association ran a function in my honour to raise some funds for the missions. If it did entail my playing for Westmeath in Gaelic Park, so be it. I would put my aging muscles and bones to the test for a good cause.

When the Mill Hill Superior in Albany heard I was in town, he contacted me and asked me to help out with mission appeals. This is a system in the USA whereby missionary societies are given permission to visit various parishes, speak of their missionary apostolate at all the Masses and take up a collection which would go to help the Society's work abroad. I agreed to help, which meant I was committed to a different parish each weekend. The busiest weekend of all was a certain date in June when I was assigned to St. Joan of Arc parish in Jackson Heights, N.Y. That weekend I preached at twelve Masses. It was a big Church with a large auditorium downstairs to cater for overflowing congregations. From 6.0 a.m. there was Mass on the hour in the Church and a quarter past the hour in the auditorium downstairs. It was hectic going but I enjoyed the challenge and the results were worth it.

Fr. Gerard Mahon, our new Superior General, was over from London. He contacted me and asked if I'd be willing to take a home appointment rather than go back to Uganda. I told him that I had already done six years in Ireland after ordination and I wanted to return to Uganda where I had settled down to life as a missionary. "Would I refuse a home appointment?" he asked. The answer was no, as after all I had taken a missionary oath of obedience. He dropped the subject. However some time later I got a nice letter from him thanking me for my willingness and appointing me as Vocations Director in the Irish Region. I was surprised and reluctantly accepted the appointment. Mentally I decided that after three years I would request a return to Uganda. My family were all happy with the appointment as I would be based near them once more.

In September 1967, I took up my new responsibilities. What does a Vocations Director do? Obviously he tries to recruit candidates for his diocese or religious congregation. How does one go about it? Ireland in the sixties was undergoing huge social changes. The advent of TV, free secondary education for all, open-ended discussion on previously 'taboo' subjects such as contraception, sexual morality and feminism, all added to a growing public debate and the challenge to think for oneself. The Catholic Church which had been such a dominant force in Irish life found it difficult to cope with the new changes and the challenges to some of its teaching. Yet it was still a powerful influence on the lives of most people. This was reflected in the number of candidates who entered seminaries and religious houses of formation at that time. In 1967 over one thousand three hundred young men and women felt they had a religious vocation and entered houses of formation. The breakdown was as follows: 291 men entered diocesan seminaries to train for the diocesan priesthood; 343 entered religious or missionary seminaries; 166 began training to be Brothers and 509 women entered different Religious Institutes of Sisters. That same year there were 364 ordinations to the priesthood in Ireland.

While these figures seem almost incredible from today's viewpoint, a decline had set in and many Bishops and Religious superiors were worried. Their response was to appoint a vocations director to recruit candidates for their own diocese or religious Institute. This led to competition and rivalry which was counter productive. Most of us felt that there was a more constructive approach where we could co-operate with one another in running retreats and open vocations workshop to help young people discern their future within the Catholic Church. This appealed to me greatly. We formed an association of Vocation Directors, called Response. We met informally, shared ideas and planned ahead. We were very much influenced by the documents of the Second Vatican Council. One read: *The task of fostering vocations devolves on the whole Christian Community which should do so in the first place by living in a full Christian way.* So vocations work is not a peripheral activity. It's at the heart of the Church, rooted in Christian family life and in Christian values promoted by school and parish.

In our approach to vocations, it was important to emphasise that Baptism was the fundamental sacrament, by which each person has a hundred per cent vocation in the Church, whether priest or religious, layman or woman. By our Baptism we are all called to the fullness of life and Christian holiness. We are all called to play our part in building up the Kingdom of Christ. Our job was to help people discern where God was calling them, to create a situation where they could think clearly about their future and make a mature decision. When sometimes I was accused of brain-washing the young, I liked to point out that we are all subject to brainwashing almost every moment of our lives, through the media, through advertisements, through friends with vested interests, in a thousand different subtle ways. The difference which I pointed out with a smile, was that I firmly believed that my detergent washed whiter than white!

It was a confusing time for priests and religious. Many were asking to be released from their vows. The most common reason was a desire to get married. Modern psychology emphasised the need for personal fulfilment and intimacy. Some of them who left were making the right decision, having entered priesthood or religious life for the wrong reasons. Some very good men and women were leaving for whatever reason. Most of us had friends who did so. It did challenge one to examine one's own motives for staying. I never thought seriously of leaving myself. I had made a life commitment and that was that. Yet sometimes the loneliness of my state hit me like a ton of bricks. I remember once visiting an old classmate, now married with a couple of young children. We had a pleasant evening together. It was a happy domestic scene, man, his wife and two children. We recalled old days together and many boyhood adventures. On my way home that night, it struck me that that simple scene would never be part of my life. When I got back to where I was based and entered my room, I never saw such a cold empty space. On occasions like this one must turn to the Master for whose sake we made our commitment and ask for all the help we need. As a missionary I always felt the celibate commitment was particularly appropriate. This was illustrated during the bad days in Uganda, when most of the overseas married Anglican ministers left for the safety of their families. Our Mill Hill missionaries stayed on through thick and thin. Some were expelled and four paid the ultimate price for their fidelity, serving their people at a time of greatest need.

Jesus Caritas Fraternity

We all need a support system. In 1974 a group of us came together to form the first Jesus Caritas Fraternity in Ireland. This is an association whose members are inspired by the spirituality of Blessed Charles de Foucauld, a French missionary priest martyred in Morocco in 1916. This emphasises deep devotion to the Blessed Sacrament, an apostolic life style and fraternal support for each other. A Fraternity consists of five or six priests who come together once a month to pray together, to review their lives in the light of the Gospel, to listen to each other and discuss problems and aspirations. We all need such a forum in which we can discuss matters of real personal importance and be assured of honest advice and support. Gradually deep friendships are formed within a fraternity. Being a member was a great blessing for me in my priestly life. I encouraged the forming of other fraternities in many dioceses and I'm happy to say the movement flourishes today.

In talking to students thinking of the priesthood, I always insisted that they give full consideration as to whether the celibate vocation was for them and whether they are mature enough to commit themselves to it. One of the finest descriptions of celibacy I found in a book written by Fr. Charles Davis, *A Question of Conscience*, after he had left the priesthood and married. This is what he wrote:

"I still regard celibacy as a meaningful vocation. I see it as the free undertaking of a privation in loving dedication to Christ. The celibate surrenders the normal human fulfilment of marriage and parenthood in order to become a sign of Christ's message of hope in a world where so many are suffering and deprived. He makes his life an expression of his faith that privation and suffering have meaning and that man's ultimate fulfilment lies deeper than ordinary human happiness".

He concludes that such a commitment is very appropriate for a priest. He also points out that celibacy must be witnessed to by a dedicated apostolic life-style. Celibacy is not a denial of love but another way of loving.

As I write this many years later I see no reason why the Church should not ordain married men in certain circumstances. In Britain we already have married priests as many Anglican ministers came over to the Catholic Church, were ordained and were allowed to continue their married status. Church structures, systems of formation and means of income might have to be changed but these difficulties should be overcome in order that a sufficient number of worthy priests are available to serve the people of God. Far better that than for the Church to tolerate some priests leading double lives, as is happening today in certain countries and is possibly more widespread than the Church would like to admit. As regards the question whether ordained priests should now be allowed to get married I can only give the answer of the wise old farmer who once told me when asked, "The Irish people would have no objection to a married clergy. What they might object to would be a courting clergy!"

As regards women priests, I have an open mind. A previous Pope, St. John Paul II, made a very definite decision on that issue and forbade further discussion. It's a complex historical and theological question whether Jesus, in choosing all male apostles, ruled out the possibility of women becoming priests. Some Scripture scholars have claimed he did not. I am happy to abide by the decision of the Church. In passing I would like to say that down the years I have met many outstanding women who would make excellent candidates if the possibility ever arose. Certainly a more active role for women in the Church should be promoted. Down the centuries women have often been the backbone of the Church and this should be acknowledged by giving them important roles of responsibility in Church structures. I once sat through a Papal audience in Rome when the Pope was surrounded by a vast array of Church dignitaries in their sartorial elegance and not a woman among them – a long way from Calvary and the first Easter.

Chapter 11
Working in my own country

I had accepted my appointment as Vocations Director on the understanding that after five years I would be allowed to return to Uganda. I always like to see the positive in any situation and I decided to make the best of my new appointment and to become involved in the local church. Besides, it was good to be back in Ireland and especially to be near my mother and family again.

I was based in our house in Dublin and had a fairly wide range of freedom as to how to go about recruiting candidates for our society. I bought a new Anglia car for £595.00. I wrote to some Bishops for permission to visit secondary schools to speak to the students about our missionary apostolate. As I mentioned already there was much competition among vocation directors in a declining market. This brought us together to form a common approach. We co-operated in running school retreats and Open Vocations Workshops. We involved laymen and women in these and were very keen to emphasise the fact that all the baptised had a full vocation in the Church, not just priests and religious. The prayer we distributed to the students focused on this. It read:

"Lord, make me a better person, more considerate towards others, more honest with myself, more faithful to you. Make me generous enough to want sincerely to do your will whatever it may be. Help me to find my true vocation in life and grant that through it, I may find happiness myself and bring happiness to others. Lord grant that those whom you call to enter the priesthood or the religious life may have the generosity to answer your call, so that those who need your help will always find it. We ask this through Christ Our Lord. Amen."

We did encourage young people who felt they might have a religious vocation to pursue the matter further and get the necessary advice so that they could discern where God was calling them. During that time I made contact with many fine young students, some of whom joined our Society and went on to become excellent missionaries.

In Ireland in the seventies the mood of young people was changing drastically. It was a time of revolt against accepted standards. Dress and hairstyles, rock music etc. were but symptoms of what was going on inside them. Traditionalists condemned the new trends without stopping to ask themselves what they signified. I never condemned the new trends even if I disliked some of them. I asked myself what they were trying to tell me and what did I as a priest have to say to these young people. I began to realise one thing quite clearly. The priesthood for them was not any definition in a catechism. It was defined by the priests they knew and sometimes the image they had formed was not very complimentary. When they asked a question, they didn't want a book answer but one that came out of my own lived experience. They challenged me to think more deeply about my own priesthood and how I lived it. I also noticed that behind a lot of the apparent rebellion of young people there was a depth of goodness and concern that needed to be channelled in the right direction or it might be dissipated in useless causes. I was often called upon to give retreats in various schools, both for boys and girls, and I always found this a very fruitful apostolate.

Chapter 12
National Director for Vocations

As already stated the vocation directors from the many religious and missionary congregations formed an Association called 'Response'. I was elected chairman. We met regularly and drew up a national plan for the promotion of religious vocations. We kept the Hierarchy informed of our activities and suggested to them that they appoint a National Director for Vocations, to co-ordinate the whole apostolate. We felt it should be a diocesan priest. By now I had done almost five years as vocations director for our Society and was planning a return to the missions. I was involved also in giving clergy retreats. In the summer of 1971 I gave the annual retreat to the priests of Armagh archdiocese, including the Archbishop, Cardinal Conway. So between talks, I had some time to discuss with him our national plan for vocations, under a National Director. He promised to bring it up at the next meeting of the Hierarchy in Maynooth. Some months later after the meeting of the Bishops he contacted me to let me know that the plan had been accepted with one proviso – namely that I would accept the job as National Director. I was a bit taken aback as I had expected the Bishops to appoint one of their own diocesan men to the job. Accepting the position would mean postponing my return to the missions. I consulted widely with my fellow vocation directors, with my Mill Hill Superior and colleagues. They all advised me to take the job as it was a vote of confidence by the Bishops in my ability to take on this new assignment. It would be for a three years term and after due reflection and prayer, I accepted the appointment.

It was something new in the Irish Church and attracted a certain amount of publicity from the national media. There were several articles in the press about the appointment and the reasons for it. My office was based at Veritas House in Lower Abbey Street, Dublin. I continued to live in our house in Dartry. I was given a job description with various terms of reference. It was very much up to myself to develop the way forward. I would do so in close co-operation with other vocation directors by way of running Open Vocations Workshops and retreats. My overall aim was Christian renewal at every level of society and particularly that any person who felt a call towards the priesthood or religious life should be provided with full information and guidance so that the person could make a mature decision.

My appointment in September 1972 was for three years. This was renewed in 1975 and again in 1978. It was nice to be assured that one was doing a reasonable job but I had not planned to spend so long at home. After all I was a missionary priest. I would be celebrating the Silver Jubilee of my priesthood in 1980 and I felt it was time I returned to the missions. So when I accepted the third term ending in 1981 I insisted that this would be my last term of office so that I would be free to return to the foreign missions.

In general I enjoyed my work as I became involved in a wide range of activities. I helped out in many parishes and gave quite a few parish missions. When I prepared for these I recalled some of the missions I had attended as a young lad when it seemed that the principal aim of the preacher was to frighten the daylights out of the congregation with all sorts of threats if they didn't repent. I'm not sure if such sermons did any good at all and they may have done a lot of damage. Two big obstacles to growth in spiritual maturity are a poor God image and a poor self image and such sermons can lead to both. The image of God that was given was of a vengeful figure prying into every area of one's life, ready to pounce if one stepped out of line. This was far from the image of God as revealed by Jesus in the Gospels. As regard self-image, there was no need to remind people of their frailty and sinfulness. They were in far greater need to be reminded of their dignity as children of a loving God, redeemed by Jesus Christ. The Good News of the Gospel is a message of love, hope and redemption. Without overlooking the challenges from so much evil around us, that was the message I always tried to preach. Walk tall. Be proud of your innate dignity. The challenge of the Christian vocation is to live lives worthy of that dignity.

I often got requests to help out in parishes with confessions when Christmas was near. Most Catholics went to confession then and sometimes on Christmas Eve I sat in the Confession box for up to three hours. It was a most fruitful apostolate. One parish priest whom I knew well asked for help in this way. "Fr. Chris, will you please come down and help with confessions before Christmas. You see, I like to have a good man around when the big fish are inclined to rise!" Indeed many who had been way from the Church for some time often came back to make their peace with God at that time. I heard more stories then than Joe Duffy on live- line could imagine. On one occasion after hours in the box, I thought I had finished but then I heard a heavy step approaching. I pulled back the slide in the darkened box and was hit with a strong smell of Guinness. I used my usual greeting: "You're very welcome". The man on the other side of the screen paused and said slowly, "Father, I was afraid you'd throw me out. I've been away for years. I'm an awful sinner. Now I don't want to take up your time so just put me down for everything!" I asked him had he ever robbed a bank. "Good God, no, why did you ask that?" I told him that he was probably not half as bad as he thought he was. The rest was easy. We had a good chat about sorrow and a new beginning. He was no angel but the black spots in his past life were easily washed away in the power of the sacrament. He remained at the back of the church afterwards to greet me. As I wished him a Happy Christmas he gave a great big smile, spat on his hand in the manner of a farmer who has made a good sale, put it out for a firm handshake and said to me, "Put it there, Father, you've made my Christmas."

Teams of Our Lady

I was also chaplain to a group of married couples belonging to a movement called Teams of Our Lady. The group of about six married couples would meet once a month in each other's homes just to share with one another on how to live their married lives in the light of the Gospel. These sessions provided a relaxed atmosphere for the participants to discuss freely serious matters of responsibilities, relationships, challenges, the ups and downs of married life in the light of their Christian faith. The chaplain would simply reflect back to them what he discerned and how the Gospel might speak to them in their daily lives. Many of the couples belonged to social clubs but all stressed that this was the one place where they could discuss serious spiritual matters and personal challenges without embarrassment. They learned a lot from each other. Close friendships grew through these meetings. As chaplain, I felt privileged to be part of this movement. My own life was enriched by gaining an insight into the responsibilities of married life, the joys and sorrows, the tensions and worries at the heart of any couple raising a family. I was also strengthened by the love and affection I experienced from these people and their families. These friendships continue right down to the present day.

Paedophilia

During the seventies I gave retreats to the clergy in many dioceses and to groups of religious personnel so I was in contact with a great number of priests and religious. I never preached down at them but shared my own experience of trying to live the Gospel in my daily life. Very many came to me for a chat or sacramental confession. I considered that an important role for me was to encourage, support and inspire. During these sessions many problems surfaced, some dealing with relationships, with drink or debts or whatever. I would like to mention in passing that never once did I hear a word of paedophilia. I was totally unaware of this evil in our midst.

Granted it concerned only a tiny minority of priests. Yet when the scandal surfaced later it left me numb with shock, especially as I knew two of the guilty ones quite well and I thought they were good priests. I never suspected a thing. I was shocked too at the neglect and slowness of some church leaders in handling the problem so that children continued to be exposed to harm. Like so many other priests I felt betrayed by the whole affair. It's easy to be wise in hindsight. On reflection I now feel that there were three factors involved. Most people, many psychiatrists among them, didn't realise how addictive the disease of paedophilia is – and it is a disease, however evil. Secondly there was poor understanding of the deep damage done to the victim and lastly, scandal was the big sin to be avoided at all costs. So the tendency was to hush the whole thing up and this led to devastating consequences. When the Murphy and Ryan reports came out I was stunned. I could never understand how anyone, least of all a priest, could perpetrate such evil.

The Media

My work as national director also entailed going on TV and radio from time to time for discussions on religious topics. Challenging questions were often posed but overall I felt the programmes were basically fair and honest. I was also asked to contribute to the Outlook programme. This was a four minute slot before the ending of the TV programmes each evening. The topics were left to oneself. It was a good opportunity to get across a Christian message. I always chose a theme relevant to the day. On the Feast of Brigid one year, when I spoke of the saint, I had as background a picture of St. Brigid's Church in Boher, my own parish, and all the locals were very proud of that. The programmes often drew quite a lot of response, especially if I had touched on a controversial topic.

Blessed Mother Teresa of Calcutta

Many enquiries from young people came into my office and I answered them all personally. This put me in touch with many wonderful people trying to discern their future. Some were inspired by well known priests and religious. Mother Teresa was famous for her work in India and some girls were interested in joining her order, Missionaries of Charity. One of the great blessings of my life was meeting Mother Teresa. I met her in Dublin and I once travelled with her from Rome to London when we had adjoining seats on the flight. While she asked me about my missionary experience I just wanted to listen to her. She certainly had a captive audience as she spoke of her work among the poor, her faith and trust in a loving God despite the many hardships in her life. One piece of advice helped me greatly in my future missionary work when faced with many problems. This is how she put it. "Many people who praise my work sometimes point out that considering the vast poverty in India, my contribution is just a drop in a bucket and so why bother? This can be very depressing. However, the Christian approach is that each day, despite all the problems, you can reach out and touch one other human being with Christ's love and compassion and that in itself is of inestimable value." What an inspiring thought from a saint and of course her own initial act of lifting a poor down-and-out from the gutter in Calcutta has touched the lives of millions and sparked off a vast apostolate. Yes, it is always better to light a single candle than to curse the darkness.

Pope John Paul 11 visits Ireland

Towards the end of the seventies we had the visit of Pope John Paul 11 to Ireland. This aroused great expectations and an intense period of preparation. On 29th September 1979 he landed at Dublin Airport, the plane first circling over the Phoenix Park where a crowd of over a million people were waiting. I'll never forget the atmosphere on that bright September morning. After preliminaries at the airport he arrived in the Park to lead in the celebration of Mass. It was a most wonderful occasion, the first visit of a Pope to Ireland and of course, this Pope was somewhat different, a man from Poland who had experienced the horrors of war, who had an outgoing manner and with a great gift of communication. The liturgy was beautiful, with a vast crowd stretching out as far as the eye could see, yet truly united with their spiritual leader in offering the one Sacrifice of the Mass.

The following day I was privileged to be on the altar with him for the Youth Mass in Galway and I'll never forget that moment when he told the young people of Ireland 'I love you'. It provoked over ten minutes of tumultuous applause. I looked down on that sea of faces and was very proud to be present on this great occasion. The three days of his visit drew huge crowds to the venues of Drogheda, Maynooth and Limerick and to the Shrine of our Lady at Knock 'the focus of my visit', to celebrate the centenary of the apparitions there. John Paul truly cast a spell over the whole country during his three day visit. There was an atmosphere of euphoria and enthusiasm. It was a high point of the Church in Ireland. Even the police who had originally expressed concern about the possibility of burglaries and other crimes, as so many of them would be tied up with crowd control, later made it known that during those three days the country was virtually crime free.

International Conference and Attempted Assassination

Towards the end of my term as National Director, in May 1981, there was a big international convention in Rome to discuss the whole question of priestly and religious vocations worldwide. Representatives from all over the world were invited. There were over three hundred delegates present consisting of Bishops, priests and sisters, with a few lay people. I was asked to lead the Irish delegation. We had concelebrated Mass with the Holy Father in St. Peter's Basilica on the Sunday. The conference proper began on

Monday morning with a plenary session in one of the spacious meeting halls in the Vatican. Each afternoon we divided into five different language groups. The English group consisted of about seventy delegates from English speaking countries around the world including some from Africa, India and the Middle East. Our first job was to elect a chairperson and secretary. Much to my surprise I was proposed, seconded and elected unanimously as chairman. I knew the agenda very well so I accepted.

On the Wednesday afternoon, a member of the Irish delegation, Fr. Cyprian Candon O.P., came to me before the meeting and asked to be excused as it was his one chance to attend a Papal Audience which was about to take place in St. Peter's Square, not far from where we were seated. I wished him well and began the meeting. It was the 13th May and the next few minutes will be riveted forever in my memory. I had begun the session, was reading out the agenda when suddenly at the back door of the hall I saw Fr. Cyprian rush in. His face was white. He shouted across the assembly, "The Pope is shot". There was consternation. People pushed back chairs and there were cries of unbelief. I called for order and asked Cyprian what had happened and what was the Pope's condition. He cried, "I don't know, I only heard the shots and saw him fall". We were all stunned being only too aware of a tragedy happening within yards of where we were. Then I heard a strong American voice, that of Bishop Mestice of New York, who said, "This is dreadful news. There is nothing further we can do here. I move that we recess immediately." They all rose and looked at me and, thank God, I had sufficient presence of mind to handle the situation. I said, "That this is terrible news, I fully agree. That there is nothing further we can do, I totally disagree. We can pray. In view of the Pope's great devotion to Mary, we will now say the Rosary that our Blessed Mother will protect him and heal him whatever his condition is " The whole assembly dropped to their knees. I led the five sorrowful mysteries. It was a prayer of intense petition. As it was ending an Italian priest appeared. I called for silence. He announced that the

Pope had reached the Gemelli Hospital. The situation was critical. He was receiving a transfusion but there was great hope. We said a joyful 'Hail, Holy Queen' and then I simply said "Now we recess".

The attempted assassination by the Turk Ali Agca cast a gloom over our assembly as it did over the whole of Rome. We followed the daily medical bulletins and prayed that the Pope would recover. We continued our meetings till the end of the week when we concluded our business and went our separate ways. It later transpired that the Pope's recovery was almost miraculous as the bullets had not touched a vital part of his body. He attributed this to Our Lady of Fatima on whose Feast day the attempted assassination took place. The Pope later visited his attacker in prison in a gesture of forgiveness and reconciliation. It was just another mark of the greatness of the John Paul II.

End of Term

My nine years as National Director for vocations were by and large challenging but enjoyable. It gave me an opportunity to serve the church in Ireland and to work with many priests, religious and laity in a variety of ways. The number of priestly and religious vocations declined but not very drastically. Twice, in 1977 and in 1980, I gave the Ordination Retreat in Maynooth. On each occasion there were up to sixty young men preparing for Ordination that year. I felt it a privilege to share with them my own experience of priesthood and encouraged them to dedication and commitment in their chosen vocation. It was always a pleasure to meet some of them in later years.

At the end of my term of office, I got many letters of thanks and appreciation from the Bishops and religious Superiors. Bishop Joseph Carroll wrote a very gracious letter on behalf of the Hierarchy and asked me to accept a generous gift "as a token of our gratitude for your outstanding work as National Director over a period of nine years". So it was pleasant to leave the job on a high note.

Chapter 13
A Sabbatical Year

A Sabbatical year is a great privilege because it gives one time to reflect and pray and do some further studies to prepare for future ministry. I had decided to spend the year in Rome where our Society has a house. I registered for courses at two Universities. In 1980 I had celebrated my Silver Jubilee, a wonderful occasion and a time to look back and look forward. The most recent years in Ireland meant I could be close to family and friends. I officiated at family weddings and baptisms and formed many new friendships. I knew it would be hard to go abroad again but at least the closest tie of all was no longer there. My mother died in 1978. She was a woman of deep simple faith and devotion and like so many mothers of that generation raised her family in difficult times with great courage and fidelity. For many years she had suffered from an ulcerated leg, the result of a neglected wound, which caused her great pain. When my brother Tom went to America in 1962, mother went to live with my sister, Teresa, and her husband Benny Moran, in Navan and this was the saving of her. Surrounded by loving care with no farmyard chickens to worry about, with grandchildren beside her, she made great progress health-wise. When I came back from Africa in 1967 I was delighted at how well she looked. I used to take her to Mass at the local Mercy Convent where she made many friends among the Sisters, especially with old Sr. Gerard. They chatted about everything. She once asked Mum to pray hard for Fr. Gilhooley's intentions. Thinking that he was some missionary priest in danger, Mum prayed for him till one day I told her that Fr. Gilhooley was none other than the manager of the Offaly football team and that Sr. Gerard's nephew, Larry Coughlin, was playing centre field for them! I think the prayers ceased.

However well Mum was cared for by Teresa and Benny, her heart was still in the old home where she had raised us all. My brother Tom with his wife, Delia, and baby daughter, Mary, were now back there and Mum longed for the day when she could join them. So in due course she returned to Killeenbrack and settled down with them in their new home. She now had Mary, a new granddaughter to care for and some time later a new grandson, Michael. During the following years she was in reasonably good health and could go on quite a few outings. The first time she attended Boher Mass after having been years in Navan, she was quite fussy about what to wear. I was the celebrant and, funnily enough, on the way over to the Church, she asked me quite a few times what to put in the collection. In the end I said to her, "O.K. Mum, if you want to impress the locals, why don't you put a fiver on the plate. Don't worry. I'll give it back to you afterwards!" She dropped the subject and there was no fiver dropped on the plate.

Death of mother

I often said Mass for Mum in the house and this she considered a great privilege. Brought up in a tradition where it was forbidden for lay people to touch the sacred vessels, after Mass I used to ask her to put away the chalice and how lovingly she did so. In May 1978, I was due to give a parish mission in Pennyburn parish in Derry. I called to see Mum on the way there and said Mass in the home. I told them I would see them on my way back. The mission lasted two weeks and proved a very busy time. On my day off during the second week, I took a trip to visit the Giants Causeway. I enjoyed the wonderful sight and sent my Mum a postcard from there. She was not destined to receive it. When I got back to Derry that evening, I received the sad news that my mother had died. It was quite a shock. The following morning with a heavy heart I headed back to the family home. Two days later I officiated at her Requiem

Mass and funeral, a privilege but also a challenge how to direct one's natural grief and sorrow into a ceremony of love and dignity. My mother, the humblest of beings, would be proud of the great turn out at the funeral Mass. The overflow congregation included over thirty priests and two Bishops. She was laid to rest beside her beloved husband, Michael, in Boher cemetery.

Rome

In mid-September, 1981, I left for Rome to begin my Sabbatical year. I went by car with Fr. John Hanley, Rector of the Irish College. It was a most pleasant journey through England, France and Italy. It took three days. We visited important places along the way, including Ars, the home of St. John Vianney, the famous Cure, where we said Mass at his Shrine. In Northern Italy we visited the ancient Monastery of Bobbio, founded by St. Columbanus and again we were privileged to say Mass at his Tomb. Driving south through spectacular scenery we eventually reached Rome and Fr. John brought me to our house in Via Innocenzo X, where I was welcomed by the Rector and colleagues. This would be my home for the next nine months. It is pleasantly situated near a spacious park and about a half hour's walk from St. Peter's Basilica.

Rome is a wonderful city. I had plenty of time to enjoy the sights, the splendid architecture and the unlimited art treasures. One could spend hours in the Sistine Chapel alone or in St. Peter's Basilica and want to come back again. Every Sunday I would visit a different site such as the Coliseum or one of the magnificent churches and ponder the incredible history of this great city. Some evenings I would take a walk across the Geniculum Hill on my way to St. Peter's. From the hill one gets a magnificent overview of the city. I would sit down and ponder the history of the beginning of Christianity here. In my mind's eye I would go back almost two thousand years and view the scene down below: the great Forum, Centre of orators and scholars, Nero's Palace, the great Roman armies returning from Gallic campaigns bringing their huge haul of booty and slaves, marching triumphantly in unconquerable mode. Then in my mind's eye at dusk one evening I would see a solitary figure quietly making his way into the city, Peter the Fisherman. He probably had his few personal belongings in a string bag. He was armed with nothing but his faith in Jesus Christ. He was coming to make contact with the few scattered Christians and facing the might of the cruel Emperor, the powerful army, the array of pagan philosophers and scholars. He would preach a new religion, a message of Redemption, Hope and Love with no soft options or compromises with the corrupt practices of the day, a message of integrity and self-sacrifice. He would survive for a very short time and be executed as a common criminal, crucified upside down and buried in an unmarked grave. A total failure, surely. Now as I look down, the Forum is a heap of ruins, the Palace of the 'divine' Caesar gone with the wind, Imperial Rome is no more but over the site of that grave once carefully tended by the few persecuted Christians stands the magnificent Basilica of St. Peter. In the great piazza on Easter Sunday there would gather over half a million Christians from every corner of the world to listen to the successor of St. Peter and to receive his blessing given Urbi et Orbi, to the city and to the world.

I didn't forget my purpose for being in Rome. I booked into some excellent courses at two universities, the Gregorianum and the Angelicum. I found them very helpful for my future ministry. They were mostly on Spiritual Direction, Counselling, Pastoral Care and Human development. I learned enough Italian to get by and say Mass for local communities. I found the Italian people most hospitable and full of the joy of living. I enjoyed my time so much that I decided to spend Christmas there rather than go back to Ireland. I found Rome quite free from all the commercial hype we experience back home. We celebrated St. Patrick's Day and other feasts with great gusto. After Easter I joined a group of Sisters on a pilgrimage to the Holy Land.

I always felt very welcome at the Irish College by the Rector, Fr. John Hanley and the Staff. I had once given a retreat to the students there so I knew the area well. The College is situated near the two great Basilicas of St. John Lateran and Mary Major. It is within walking distance of the Coliseum and also near the church of the Irish Dominicans, San Clemmente. This is one of the most interesting sites in Rome, not to be missed. Underneath the present 12th century church excavations revealed the pillars and framework of a 4th century church and underneath that again a first century Roman street with a pagan shrine to Mithras, the Persian god of light. The ashes seen there could be from the great fire of Rome started by Nero.

Mass with John Paul II

The most memorable occasion of my time in Rome was concelebrating Holy Mass with Pope John Paul II in his private oratory in the Vatican. The Pope always liked to have a small community with him for morning Mass and I was fortunate to be invited to join him on the morning of 3rd January. His secretary, Fr. John McGee, who arranged it told me to be at the bronze door at 6.45 a.m. I was there in plenty of time. It was a crisp clear morning. I walked briskly around under the shadows of Bernini's giant columns for about ten minutes. I went over to the great bronze door and found nobody there. Then it dawned on me that they were all inside. Yes indeed, an expectant, hushed, happy group waiting to be led up to the papal apartments. The group included Fr. Robert Nash, the well known Jesuit priest, author and preacher, celebrating his Golden Jubilee, three other priests, five Irish Dominican nuns and about fifteen laymen and women, including a newly married couple and some of the helpers who serve at Knock Shrine.

A Swiss guard checked us through and another led us up the stairs, then out into a courtyard, up a further set of stairs and we waited at a large mahogany door. We waited in silence for about five minutes. Then Fr. McGee opened the door and quietly motioned us inside. We crossed a short passage and we were in a beautiful reception room. Some of the group had brought gifts and various presentations for the Pope and were asked to leave them there. We priests went into the Sacristy to vest. As I passed the open door of the beautiful oratory, I saw John Paul kneeling there before the Blessed Sacrament. He had been there since six o'clock and this was his routine each morning.

We vested for Mass and moved quietly into our seats beside the altar. The rest of the group were already seated. The Holy Father was still kneeling in prayer. Then he rose slowly and vested at the altar and began the Mass. His English was slow and very deliberate and that rich baritone voice evoked memories of his days in Ireland. He looked so much older now, no wonder, two and a half years further on bearing the burdens of office and surviving an assassin's bullets. My heart goes out to him. It is impossible not to be moved. A young man read the Epistle. The Sisters led the choir. I read the Gospel. We all sat down and reflected for a considerable time. At the Offertory the Pope was assisted at the altar by his two secretaries. Then as all the priests gathered round the altar for the Canon of the Mass, the two secretaries graciously moved to the side and allowed us the places next the Pope. Fr. Nash was on his right and I on his immediate left and I turned the pages for him as he carefully followed the English text. It was easy to concelebrate with him, so relaxed and dignified. At the consecration, he raised the host, then the chalice and we bowed in silent adoration. At the sign of peace he turned and embraced me. 'Pax tecum', 'Et cum spiritu tuo'. Then on to Holy Communion and we paused afterwards for silent thanksgiving.

After Mass we were ushered into the reception room. Fr. McGee arranged us in some sort of order. The Holy Father entered and began his round of greetings. Fr. Nash was first and was congratulated on his Golden Jubilee. He had a book for the Pope and a whole list of people to be prayed for. 'Certainly, certainly' said the Pope. Then he came to me. I bowed and kissed his outstretched hand. Fr. McGee introduced me to the Pope and told him that I was National Director of Vocations for Ireland. "Haven't you come a long way for vocations," the Pope said with a mischievous smile. I took up the point and said simply, "Your Holiness, I'm going much farther, back to Uganda later this year. Won't you pray for me" "Indeed, I will," he said. I told him that I prayed for him each day and that I had offered Holy Mass that morning for peace in his beloved Poland. This was a time of tension in Poland between the trade union movement, Solidarity, and the communist government. He grasped my arm tightly and said, "Thank you. I really appreciate that." I had many things to say to him, greetings from my family in Ireland, from my community, from the people of my parish of Ballymore/Boher. I'm not sure if I got everything in and what matter. Prepared tidy little speeches tend to get lost on such occasions. What did matter was two people present to each other, a priest reaching out with a great sense of affection and loyalty to the Vicar of Christ and the Pope reaching out with fatherly care to one of the least of his brothers in Christ.

The magic few moments were soon over and he had moved on to the next in line, a young priest from Kerry and then on to each of the group present. The Pope gave each of us a Rosary beads. At the end he seemed reluctant to leave. I spoke to him again. He made himself available for more photographs. Different groups formed. The priest from Kerry asked me to suggest a formal picture with just the priests. "Certainly", he said and we gathered near him. He was totally available with no sign of fussiness or impatience. As the nuns and others rearranged themselves he looked on with mild amusement. At the end he moved out slowly. We said our farewells, gave him a final clap as he passed back to his own apartment. No, he didn't ask us to join him for breakfast, although he had been known to do so for some very surprised guests!

I couldn't help thinking of this man with the cares of the world on his shoulders, with the immediate problems of Poland weighing very much upon him, with all the urgent pressing problems facing him, yet finding time for us all as if he hadn't a care in the world. After breakfast he would return to his study to scan his appointments for the day, to work on his many sermons, addresses and speeches. At 10.30 he would begin his more open day, meeting public figures and advisers, making innumerable decisions in promoting the welfare of Christ and the Church. This was a man who had defied the two greatest evils of the 20th century, Nazism and Communism and had prevailed. Now as leader of the Church he was defying the soft options of modernity and relativism, insisting on the objective values of truth, goodness and beauty and telling the people that they were nothing without God and that true religion demanded courage, self-sacrifice and reaching out to all in need. He insisted on deep thought and the value of suffering. He was truly one of the greatest moral leaders of the 20th century. It was a privilege to have shared that morning with him.

Afterwards we descended those steps down from the papal apartments and into the fitful sunshine of a Roman January morning. With a couple of the other priests, I went into the nearest snack-bar for a cup of coffee and a sandwich. We all felt great, elated for the experience had surpassed all our expectations. It confirmed me in my priesthood and left me with treasured memories.

Farewell to Rome

My term in Rome ended in June. I had a busy time finishing courses and doing the required exams. I got in some more travel, visiting locations such as Sienna, made famous by St. Catherine and Assisi, the home of the great St. Francis. Soon it was time to prepare for my return to Ireland to take a summer break before returning to Uganda. I had been in close contact with my colleagues in Uganda who assured me of a great welcome when I returned. Many missionaries had been expelled during the dreadful years of Idi Amin so it was good to have someone returning. I had made many friends in Rome, a city of endless attractions and it was a bit of a wrench to leave. Fr. Martin Drennan, who was spiritual director at the Irish College at the time and a close friend, invited me to accompany him on his return to Ireland by car. As on the way to Rome, the return journey home was equally interesting and we called to many places of Christian interest including Taize. This is the great centre of ecumenical prayer in France. It was established by Bro. Roger during the war and continues to attract thousands of young people from around the world. Eventually we were back in Ireland. I had planned to spend some time with my family, pay a visit to the States and then return Africa.

Chapter 14
Return to Africa

I was asked by my Society Superior if I would be willing to return to Uganda when I had completed my present commitment in 1981 as Bishop Odongo of Tororo diocese had asked for me. I immediately agreed. When it was suggested that I should take some time before making a decision considering the troubled situation in Uganda then, I remarked that if I considered the matter too long the answer might be no. It was good to make a quick decision and plan accordingly. The summer of 1982 went by quickly. I did a stint in the States helping out with mission appeals and saying goodbye to family and friends there. Back in Ireland there were plenty of goodbyes and a final farewell party in Boher Hall. It was quite a wrench leaving Ireland after several happy years but I felt it was the right thing to do. My Mill Hill colleagues in Dublin wished me well and in early October I took the boat from the North Wall in Dublin with quite a few boxes of goods for Uganda. These would be conveyed by container from Mill Hill London. On 10th October I flew to Nairobi, made my way by car to Kisumu and was collected from there by an old friend and colleague from Uganda, Fr. Jim Daley.

On October 13th we crossed from Kenya back into Uganda. The border itself which I had remembered as a quiet place was now a shambles of activity, a lot of cars, trucks, bicycles and people with animals everywhere. There were two border posts, plenty of officials checking car registrations, engine numbers, contents of luggage, etc. but eventually we got through. Tororo Rock, a massive two hundred feet high rock jutting up out of the ground, loomed ahead, a very distinctive feature of the landscape. I had been away for fifteen years. Uganda was now a changed country, utterly devastated after years of Idi Amin misrule.

The Idi Amin years

Idi Amin had been a sergeant in the old colonial army, the King's African Rifles. When Uganda got independence in October 1962 he was promoted far beyond his ability and finally became commander of the Ugandan army. The President, Milton Obote, felt Amin would be for ever grateful for the promotion and would be too incompetent to lead a coup. He was wrong. Amin led a coup in 1971 when Obote was attending a Commonwealth Conference in Singapore. In the beginning Western powers viewed Amin as a figure of fun. He offered to become King of Scotland. He sent a message of support to Nixon during the Watergate scandal. He advised Syria how to recapture the Golan Heights. He awarded himself so many honours that he had a special jacket made on which to pin all the medals! Behind it all he was a ruthless monster probably responsible for half a million deaths as his ill-disciplined soldiers did what they liked.

In 1972 he expelled all the Asians. These numbered some eighty thousand and they were the backbone of the economy. The first of them had come to Uganda to work at the building of the railway system from the coast town of Mombasa right up to KAMPALA. They remained on and contributed much to the country. They ran tea and coffee estates. Their well-stocked 'dhukas' (small retail shops) could be found in most trading centres. They ran garages, imported cars and supplied building materials to many mission centres. Our missionaries had many dealings with them and found them very helpful. In 1972 Amin, in one of his moments of madness, claimed he had had a dream and decided to expel all Asians. He was driven by greed as he felt he could amass a fortune from their properties which they were forced to abandon. They were allowed to take with them only a few items of personal value. The rich ones, foreseeing something like this, managed to get their money out of the country. Many of the less well-off were left in dire straits as they packed a few personal items and headed for the airport. Whatever little jewellery the women had was looted by soldiers at the many roadblocks. Tragic tales emerged such as that of one family who, driven to despair by all the harassment, simply drove their car into the Nile river in a mass suicide. With the departure of the Asians Uganda's economy totally collapsed and there was widespread corruption and looting   Britain to its credit helped many of the deported Asians. Our own Society offered free accommodation for several months to a large group of them.

In 1979 Amin made the mistake of allowing his troops to plunder and pillage part of neighbouring Tanzania. The President of that country, Julius Nyrere, a man of great courage and integrity, who had publicly rebuked Amin, ordered his troops to drive the invaders out and then in answer to many appeals decided to liberate Uganda. His troops did this over a short period and Obote returned as President. Amin, a typical bully, fled at the first sign of danger and sought refuge in Jeddah in Saudi Arabia where he died some years later.

Readjusting to the changes

As I entered Uganda that day in October 1982, I had many concerns and reservations. The weather matched my mood. There was no sunshine and a violent tropical thunderstorm broke over us. We drove through sheets of rain along a potholed road, past boarded up shops in the trading centre. We saw burnt out vehicles, reminders of the recent war. Amid a downpour I arrived at Tororo College in the late afternoon. Here I got a great welcome from a few missionary colleagues who had come to greet me. It helped to dispel a certain sinking feeling. I was given a room in the College. This would be my base for some time to come.

Next morning the rains had cleared. There was beautiful tropical sunshine and things looked much better. Still I felt a stranger in a country I once knew so well. I took a walk down to the town of Tororo, once a thriving trading centre with a railway station, bus park and many busy shops. Now most of the shops were boarded up. I went into one still open. It had been owned by an Indian trader. In my first tour one could buy almost anything there from clothes to sports equipment to household goods. The first thing I saw on entering were rows and rows of empty shelves except for two. One of these had rows of toilet rolls! The other had over fifty bottles of Scotch whiskey of good quality, all going cheap. Amin had imported enough booze to keep his army in a good mood and this load had somehow reached here when Amin fell. It was rather a ludicrous sight amid all the scenes of poverty.

After the overthrow of Amin there were great expectations that things would return to some sort of normality. It was not to be. When the Tanzanian army left, Obote was installed as president again. He recruited his own army but many of these were poorly trained. Sadly the pattern of violence and robbery continued often perpetrated by men in uniform. These men could often loot and pillage with impunity, sometimes under the guise of searching for guerrillas. Shortly after I came back one of our mission stations was raided by such men, using an army truck. They stole all our supplies of blankets and medicines which were about to be distributed to the poor of the area. Fear prevailed everywhere. Many villages near Kampala, the capital, were deserted. Kampala itself after dark was quite empty. It was dangerous to go out at night. To show any signs of prosperity was to make oneself a target for a criminal raid.

Sources of inspiration

Was I feeling depressed on my return? Inevitably, it was hard to avoid such feelings especially when comparing the conditions with those of my first mission tour. Yet such feelings didn't last too long.

To feel a great sense of inspiration one had only to visit Nsambya hospital in Kampala, run by the Kevinite Sisters, mostly Irish (Headquarters: Mt. Oliver, Dundalk) and see what they were doing for countless wounded and sick patients and giving shelter to refugees at night. One could call on any mission station run by the White Fathers, Comboni or our own Mill Hill Missionaries and witness their dedicated service to the poor and the needy. Here were people doing tremendous work in spite of the difficult conditions, running all sorts of projects, often working side by side with their African colleagues, bringing help to the poorest of the poor. They were wont not to dwell too much on what they had been through. Yet past tragic events were fresh in their memories. Two of our priests in Tororo diocese had been murdered by bandits; three others were wounded in cross fire; some had their cars taken at gun-point and their property looted; some had spent nights in prison. Yet morale was high. The overall approach was to get on with the job and do what had to be done, trying to bring the healing presence of Christ into a turbulent situation. I considered it a privilege to join them. Some thanked me for coming back in these circumstances but I felt they were the ones who had borne the burden of the heat during the Amin years.

It took quite a while to get things sorted out. I was anxious to study one of the local languages again so that I could help out in pastoral work. After such a long absence, my knowledge of it was decidedly rusty. I went to Kampala to get a five year work permit. The old immigration offices were very dilapidated but I was surprised that they were able to unearth my old file and I had no trouble with my request. I also renewed my driver's license. The Nissan car I had ordered had arrived in Mombasa and I went down by bus, three hundred miles, to collect it. I drove it back in easy stages, renewing acquaintance with many mission stations on the way. I was now anxious to get down to work. My main appointment was for the spiritual renewal of priests and religious and I had already got many requests for retreats and conferences. I was keen to help out in the local parish with Mass and the Sacraments because that is one way of getting close to the people and seeing their needs. Towards the end of the year I was asked to go to Pallisa, a big parish some 60 miles north of Tororo to help the local African priest there over the Christmas period. I was delighted. It was a parish I knew quite well from my previous tour. There would be plenty to do and I felt that I had truly arrived back on mission soil.

Chapter 15
Christmas in Pallisa

The 20th December saw me heading north to Pallisa in my new car with a full tank of petrol. It was many years since I celebrated Christmas in Africa and I looked forward to the work, Masses, confessions and baptisms and meeting up with old friends again. I reached Pallisa in the evening. The car was covered with dust as the last 35 miles was on a road of hard brown clay known locally as murram. I drove round the village to find the road leading to the Catholic mission which is about a mile away. The village looked in poor shape. Since the Asians left, the mosque and Hindu temple were deserted, used occasionally as recreation centres. I got out of the car and walked around. The locals greet me. One of them pointed out that I had a flat tyre. Surely not, I thought, the car's new. However the left rear tyre was as flat as a pancake. I had picked up a nail and as I set about changing the wheel I felt that there was not much chance of repairs in this sleepy hollow. I was wrong. Four men sitting around all came to help me. The wheel with the flat tyre was removed and replaced by the spare. The offending nail was found and the local garage repaired the tube. All was done in half an hour. They also washed the heavy brown dust off my car. I offered to pay. "Oh Father, we wouldn't charge you. You've come to help us for Christmas. We are all Christians here. You are most welcome."

This was the beginning of a great Christmas. I had some misgivings. I had been away for so long and my knowledge of the local language was rather rusty. I need not have worried. Fr. George, a young African priest was now the only priest in this parish of 25,000 Catholics. He had a great welcome for me. Later on we sat down and he suggested the various out-stations I would visit in the days leading up to Christmas. These visits would entail hearing confessions, Mass and baptisms. At each venue the local Catechist would assemble the Christians. I would pray with them, help them with an examination of conscience and then make myself available for individual confession. Each penitent would go back to the group where the Catechist would continue leading them in prayer. At the end I would give them all general absolution. When you have several hundred waiting for confession, what more can one do?

On Christmas Day, I said Mass in three different locations, the first at 8.0 a.m. Mass was celebrated in the open to accommodate the huge crowds, with the altar under a big mango tree for shade as Christmas comes during the hot dry season. Africans love to celebrate. They sang many hymns, organised a huge Offertory procession and time was of little consequence. The Mass lasted over an hour and a half. My only concern was to get to the next station in time for ten o'clock. The last Mass in the farthest outstation was scheduled for 12.0 noon. It was past 2.0 p.m. when I finished. The people all gathered round. They all wanted to greet the priest. I had been going since early morning and longed for a cold drink but that had to wait till I greeted all those people. I knew the Catechist would have prepared a meal for me but where is he? Then I saw him with a small delegation from a neighbouring village. They had a special request. "Father, we want you to come and bless our Crib". You feel like telling them to give you a break after such a busy morning but the only proper answer is: "How wonderful of you to have made a Crib. Where is it?" We travelled down a dusty path and reached the compound where the Crib had been erected. They had put a lot of work into it. Baby Jesus was in the centre, guarded by St. Joseph and some shepherds. There were various animals in the background but there was one grave omission: there was no Blessed Mother. Obviously her statue was lost or broken. However,

Africans are good at improvisation. Someone had found an old colour magazine and cut out a picture of a beautiful lady and pinned it at the back of the Crib to represent Mary. As I blest that Crib I had to suppress a smile. I was the only one who recognised who the lady was. It was an early picture of Marilyn Munroe! So I gave Marilyn a few extra drops of holy water and said a prayer for her. God bless you, Marilyn, you're playing a star role here today. In a way, I felt it was what Christmas is all about. Nobody is outside the embrace of God's love made visible in the person of Jesus, our Saviour.

Eventually we reached the Catechist's house. A big mud hut had been swept and garnished and prepared for the meal. There was a solid table, a chair for the Father, stools for the others. Firstly, all must greet the Father. I have never lost my appreciation of the exquisite courtesy with which the Africans, especially the women, greet a visitor. One aspect of it made me squirm a little at first when a woman kneels before you. My instinct was to protest but it is traditional in many places, so one got used to it   Children kneel before their elders. For them it is a beautiful gesture of respect. The dinner was a great affair with plenty of dishes. We had matoke (local plantain), sweet potatoes, Irish potatoes (yes, that's what they are called) and a big dish of meat and chicken. There was the ritual washing of hands, then all set to with fingers! I did manage to get the one fork available. The principle guest is always handed the gizzard, as the most tasty bit of all. We all sat around and had our fill. We talked of local events, of how Christmas is celebrated in other places, of anything and everything. Many visitors came to greet the Father. The humble surroundings were more than compensated for by the marvellous hospitality, the kindness and the courtesy of these people. I felt really at home and closer to Bethlehem than on many Christmases celebrated in more affluent surroundings.

Later the ajon (local beer brewed from millet) was produced. We sat around a big communal pot and straws were handed round.

Easy there, Christopher, you have to drive home! Actually my temperance is motivated more by taste than by self-discipline. Still the courtesies had to be observed so they handed me one of those straws. Ugh! The conversation flowed freely and many exciting tales were told around the beer pot. The sun was now going down. In the tropics there is a short twilight, 6.30 to 7.0 pm. I felt I must get back to the mission. There was a special request for me. Would I please take a pregnant woman who was about to give birth to the local hospital near the mission? Certainly, I'd be delighted. So I drove back to Pallisa this time being extra careful of the bumps on the road as I was carrying a special passenger or rather two. We arrived safely. The woman was most grateful. "If it's a boy, I'll call him Christopher," she told me.

There was a large convent attached to the mission and I was staying in the chaplain's quarters, a simple bed-sit with a shower and toilet nearby. There was a community of over twenty five sisters and it was refreshing to see so many young faces among them. The Order was founded by Mother Kevin from Co. Wicklow and was flourishing throughout Uganda and Kenya. The Sisters couldn't have been more welcoming. Happy Christmas, how did everything go? Here are some cards for you and a couple of small gifts. I was very touched by it all. I had a short rest, a quick shower and I felt quite refreshed. I joined the Sisters for evening prayer and afterwards for a light repast. The electric power had gone so we used candles which created a real Christmas atmosphere.

Later that night when all was quiet, I walked in the darkness towards the public road, past the banana plantation. In the still night air one could hear the sound of drums and singing coming from several centres, a sure sign that there was peace in this area. Everybody, Christian, Muslim and pagan alike celebrate Christmas. They celebrate and make merry as people do all over the world. It is truly right and fitting because on this day many, many years ago, the Word became flesh and pitched His tent among us and His life and love still throb in the hearts of men and women and inspire them to acts of love, greatness and heroism. In the silence of the night I said a prayer of thanksgiving for my vocation, knowing that I had regained my missionary soul that Christmas at Pallisa.

Chapter 16
An unexpected sad interlude

When I was leaving Ireland in October some friends were predicting that I'd be back within a year. No way, I promised them, not for at least three years. Little did I know what lay ahead, two deaths in the family. As already related Dad and Mum had 6 children. The eldest, Catherine, became a nun with the Little Sisters of the Assumption and I, the youngest, a priest with the Mill Hill Missionaries. The four in between, Thomas, Mary Jane, Michael and Teresa were all happily married with nineteen children between them. We were all very united and as the youngest I looked up to them all and was very close to them. I was very proud when we were all together at my Silver Jubilee celebration in Boher in 1980, Michael coming from New York and Catherine coming from Birmingham. I felt there would be many future occasions for such reunions. We were all relatively young, strong and healthy. I was sad saying goodbye on going back to Africa but my parting words were "I'll see you again in three years time".

I was now settling back to life in Uganda and planning a busy year ahead. Early in January I got word from home that my brother, Tom, was taken to hospital. I felt it couldn't be anything serious as he was such a strong man. I was wrong. He had cancer of the lungs and it was terminal. The news shocked me. He was only 62 and his overall health had always been very good. Yes, he smoked, but not that heavily, although I had often tried to persuade him to give up the habit. Now came this tragic news. I knew I'd have to go home to be with him and Delia, his wife and their two children, Mary and Michael, at this sad time. I had to decide when to travel. Perhaps he would respond to treatment and get a good remission. I decided to go home in March. It was a sad homecoming. Tom had been a great support to me all during my student days. When he heard that I was returning he told some neighbours, "Fr. Christy is coming home. He'll either cure me or bury me". Would to God I could do the former. The first evening we were alone together he asked me directly to tell him if there was any hope. Up to now the definitive truth had been shielded from him. Yes, he knew he was very ill but still hoped against hope. I was faced with a dilemma either to continue the pretence or tell him outright. I chose what I thought was right. I simply said to him, "I'm sorry Tom, the doctor said there is no hope." There was a long pause and then he asked, "How long have I got?" "About a week; did you not know?" "Of course I knew," he said. Yet I felt I had broken the last slender thread of hope. It was very painful. His wife, Delia, even asked me did I have to do it. In hindsight I'm sure it was the right thing to do. He faced up to reality with typical courage. He talked to his wife and children with words he would not otherwise have used. It cleared the air. I said Mass at his bedside every evening and gave him Holy Communion with the prayer: "Tom, my beloved brother, may the Bread of Life bring you safely unto everlasting life."

Tom died on the morning of 29th March, 1983 in the presence of his wife, Sr. Catherine and myself. At his passing, Delia, whose heart must have been broken, whispered to me, "I never knew death could be so peaceful." We remained in silent prayer for quite a long period. Then it was time for action, to inform the relatives, including Michael in New York and to make the many arrangements. I collected the two children from school, Michael from Boher primary school and Mary from Moate Mercy secondary school. I informed Fr. Conway, the parish priest, the undertaker and all the neighbours. We had the traditional Irish wake and then after two days the funeral Mass and burial in the local cemetery. A huge crowd gave a fond and fitting farewell to a very popular man. It was Holy Week, an appropriate time to reflect on the mystery of life, death and resurrection. My brother, Mike, stayed on for a couple of days and then had to return to New York. I saw him off with our usual brotherly hug and punch in the ribs. "I'll see you in two years time," were my last words to him, little knowing that Michael also would be dead before the year was out.

I had intended to take an extra week or two before returning to Uganda. I was staying with Fr. Conway in the parochial house in Ballymore. At two o'clock one morning he knocked on my door and came in looking in poor shape. We rang the local doctor who checked his heart and immediately rang the county hospital in Mullingar. Very soon I was speeding through Killare on my way to the hospital with him. A doctor was ready to receive him and gave him immediate medical help. He was to remain there for a considerable period of time followed by some further weeks of rest in Athlone. So it happened that I was asked to take charge of my own parish of Ballymore/Boher for about three months and I was happy to do so. There were even rumours that I might be appointed there if Fr. Conway did not recover. I was amused when I heard this as I had already booked my ticket back to Uganda. When Fr. Conway was ready to come back the parish gave a great farewell party in the Community Centre to show their appreciation of my help. There followed another series of farewells and at the end of June I was back in Uganda.

I had a fairly busy time ahead of me, some parish work, a programme of formation to groups of religious Sisters, retreats and conferences and I was happy to be settling down again. Then in November I got more bad news. My brother Mike in New York had taken ill and the medical report didn't look good. I couldn't believe it. Communication with New York was difficult. It sometimes took me three hours to get through on the phone to the family. We adopted another plan. I would be at a certain location at a certain time and one of the family would ring me. That worked fairly well and I was even able to talk to Mike in the hospital. Mike was very close to me and we had a common love of sport. We had played together on the Boher football team. Although very ill he assured me that he was determined to walk out of the hospital. I told him I would be there to greet him. In early December, I had arranged to speak to Mary, Mike's daughter. I was at the Bishop's House, Mbale, at a certain time on a certain date. We spoke at length. Mike was holding his own. I was hoping to travel over to New York at Christmas to be with the family. I told Mary that I was going up country for eight days and would be out of reach for that time. If anything happened she should ring this number and the Bishop would get word to me. I would be back to receive her call eight days from then. No news during those eight days was good news – or so I thought – after which I was back in Bishop's house waiting for Mary's call. Then the houseboy came in, a young adult, who told me that Mary had rung over a week ago, that he had taken the call, that my brother had died and that he had forgotten to tell anyone. I was stunned and shocked and angry. News of a death in any culture is sacred. In Africa they will go to any length to send the news. Now here was this man simply saying that he had forgotten. I felt shattered. The Bishop came in and tried to console me. When Mary did ring she told me the family were worried about me, not having got any response. I told her that I had received the sad news only half an hour before. Mike had died on 11th December, 1983. That year was one of the saddest years of my life.

When I went to New York in the summer of '85, one of the first places I visited was Mike's grave in the great cemetery called Calvary. As I prayed there one could easily look up and see the Long Island expressway. I thought of the number of times I travelled with Mike by car on our way into Manhattan. Marlboro cigarette company used to run a big advertisement saying, "You are now entering Marlboro country". Mike often joked as we looked down from the expressway that the cemetery was the real Marlboro country. Yes indeed, my brother Mike, a strong man and great footballer, was also a victim of smoking, dying at the age of 59, leaving behind his loving wife, Peggy, and six children.

Chapter 17
A few thoughts on Mission in Africa

Returning to Africa after an absence of several years gives one an opportunity to reflect on the changes that have taken place, on the different approaches to mission and the changing personnel. In the sixties our Society had over two hundred missionaries in Uganda. In the eighties we had less than fifty. Previously we had occupied most posts of importance including that of Bishop in the dioceses where we worked; now these were occupied by the local clergy. We were now servants of the local church. This was real progress. Our founder, Cardinal Vaughan, had always stressed that we should establish the Church and then move on. That is precisely what our early missionaries did. Many of them were asked to take charge of huge areas which had little or no facilities. They built churches, schools and mission hospitals for the benefit of the people. The big mission compound became a feature in many places. People came there in numbers to have their spiritual and bodily needs met. The best schools at secondary level were established by the missionaries. In Uganda there was always great rivalry between schools run by our society, such as Tororo College and Namilyango College and schools established by The Church Missionary Society (Anglican), competing at both academic and sporting levels. There was always the danger of strong Western influence with not enough emphasis on local culture. Missionaries who came in the wake of the colonial expansion in Africa were often seen as part of this Western influence. All these factors often led to a paternalistic, clerical, authoritarian Church, despite the goodness of many missionaries.

The documents of the second Vatican Council held in Rome

(1962-65) helped to prepare the way for many changes. Key words emerged such as *inculturation* and *conscientisation*. The missionary must become steeped in the local culture as the Christian message can never take deep root until it can integrate the real values of the local culture. The whole thrust of the missionary church broadened from just planting the Church and saving souls to the wider field of human rights and the dignity of the human person, a new emphasis on social justice and a preferential option for the poor and the marginalized. In my experience Catholic missionaries had always tried to help the poor but more emphasis must now be given to challenging structures of injustice and corruption at every level. The fight for human rights and social justice must be part of any programme of evangelisation. In preaching the Gospel we must see ourselves as helping people to reflect on the profound mystery of God and the mystery of humanity. We preach that Jesus is the ultimate expression of that God who has been revealing Himself in countless ways to human beings down the centuries. The teaching of Jesus must take root in the local culture. In one sense the universal Church becomes local and the local Church becomes universal. A theology of revelation must take full account of the human experience of people and its cultural expression. Obviously certain practices have to be examined in the light of the teaching of Jesus and this applies to people in every culture. The Church in Africa must have a distinct African character and as such it enriches the universal Church.

Our missionaries paid attention to the new understanding of their apostolate but in practical terms it didn't greatly alter their work and lifestyle. They had always been on the side of the poor and had done much to alleviate poverty by way of local development and establishing clinics and schools. The mission station was always a source of help to those in need. Missionaries consistently highlighted the many problems faced by those involved in healthcare and education. The fight against the dreaded disease of leprosy in Uganda was pioneered by the Franciscan Sisters led by the famous Mother Kevin. Many missionaries imported containers with vast quantities of clothing, blankets and medical supplies for distribution to the most needy. During the bad days in Uganda the missionaries were a great source of help and comfort to people in trouble. Their very presence alone was a message of support and assurance to people that they were not forgotten.

The greatest difficulty which we faced in Uganda in the eighties was political instability. As already noted, the monstrous reign of Idi Amin ended in 1979 when the Tanzanian army aided by a small group of Uganda exiles ousted him. The previous president, Milton Obote, was restored to power. Obote filled his cabinet and important army positions with his fellow tribesmen and friends. Instability and corruption continued. Two of our priests lost their lives during this period. Fr. Richard Tauber was shot dead by an army man when he refused to hand over the keys of his pick-up. Fr. George McGrath was caught in crossfire when Mbale College was attacked by robbers. It was a tough time to live through. Supplies were scarce and one had to cross the border to Kenya to get necessary provisions such as bread, sugar, salt and soap.

Meanwhile the army commander, Oyeta Ojok, was enforcing his authority. He demanded to be appointed chairman of the coffee marketing board. Coffee is the one great cash crop of Uganda, amounting to about eighty-five percent of all exports. The producers were not paid under Amin who grabbed all the money. This led to a vast amount of smuggling of bags of coffee beans to Kenya where it would fetch a reasonable price. The most common method was to use the oil tankers returning to Kenya after delivering petrol to Uganda, and pack the empty tankers with bags of coffee beans. People made a fortune in the smuggling business. They became known as the 'mafuti mingi' men! ('Much oil men' meaning wealth acquired by smuggling). Ojok, the commander of the army wanted to get his hands on the money raised from coffee and it was obvious he had other ambitions. This was all ended when he mysteriously died in a helicopter crash. It was interesting to see many important people who hated Ojok rushing to attend his funeral, a sort of public witness that they had nothing to do with his death.

A welcome visit

Through it all, life went on. Most local people survived on subsistence living, just growing enough food to sustain themselves and their families. We got used to the pot-holed roads and the many road-blocks, with soldiers placed there under the pretence of security but in reality to rip people off. By and large missionaries were respected by all sides as we were there for the good of the people. My two sisters, Sr. Catherine and Teresa, came out to visit me in 1984 and I was able to take them round without any great difficulty. We did the tourist bit, Kenya and the coast, visited the game parks and saw a huge variety of wildlife. They enjoyed it all but what left a lasting impression was the great hospitality they received everywhere especially when coming with me to visit families and various communities. They saw how the average Uganda family lived, the problems they faced, their local customs, but what touched them most was the exquisite warmth, graciousness and hospitality they received even in the humblest of surroundings. On one occasion, when visiting a poor family, I saw the mother nodding towards her young son who quietly slipped out the door. Out of the corner of my eye I could see him chasing the biggest hen in the yard. He caught it and brought it to his mother who proudly presented it to Sr. Catherine. My sister had tears in her eyes at the beautiful gesture. I told her she had to accept the hen as she was a visitor and their custom was to offer a gift.

We stayed with the Franciscan Sisters at Nsambya hospital one evening. Sr. Veronica Mary Cotter (from Cork) took my sisters on a tour of the hospital and showed them the various crowded wards. What really upset my sisters was to see the thousands of people who crowded inside the walls of the hospital after dark just for safety.

They would leave in the morning, but it was a sad reflection on the state of security in the country.

Sr. Veronica Mary was a legend in Uganda, a brilliant surgeon and gynaecologist who saved endless lives by her tireless work in the hospital. On one occasion when I was staying there I noticed that she looked very tired at morning Mass. When I asked her at breakfast if she was well, she admitted that she had spent several hours during the night in the theatre operating on wounded people. "How do you do it?" I asked. "Sure there was a great show on", she smiled. Whereupon one sister wisecracked, "I bet they all came out in stitches!" We all laughed but what was obvious was the dedication and morale of all who ministered in that hospital.

My sisters remained with me for four weeks. We visited many locations including the Shrine at Namagongo where twenty two Ugandans were martyred for their faith in the years 1886-87. We visited some communities of African nuns and my sisters were impressed to see so many young faces among them. The warmth of the welcome we got was always so genuine and sincere. Attending the parish Mass on Sunday was a special treat. Africans love to celebrate and all join in the singing. There is real active participation of all the congregation. The Mass is a joyful celebration of the Faith and time is of little importance. It's no wonder that returned missionaries often find the Sunday liturgy in some Irish parishes so dull and uninspiring. We visited Baluba where there was a leper hospital under the care of the Franciscan Sisters. I sometimes said Mass for the lepers and was always impressed by their courage and resilience. The hospital got generous funding from Germany and the disease can now be treated effectively. After four interesting weeks it was time for my sisters to leave for home. There were many farewells and they left with memories that will last a lifetime.

Chapter 18
The gathering storm

At the beginning of 1985 it was fairly clear that President Obote's regime was in trouble. One of his team who had helped him return to power became disillusioned with the rampant corruption and left the government and, as they say, went "into the bush". He was Yoweri Museveni who went back to his own tribal stronghold in the southwest of the country and began organising his own army. He had received some military training while in exile and knew well what he was doing. He approached many of the Baganda tribe who had suffered under both Amin and Obote and invited them to join his army to seek retribution. He got a good response and quietly planned a long term campaign. He was financed by Gaddafi of Libya. Meanwhile two of Obote's military generals (both called Okello) felt they were not getting enough share of the spoils available and planned to oust Obote. The upshot was another military coup. Obote with a few of his henchmen fled the country and was eventually offered asylum in Zambia. It didn't make a great difference to the ordinary people who still had to contend with poverty, corruption and political instability. Meanwhile Museveni was gaining strength in the west. The Kenya government tried to bring the various factions together at a meeting in Nairobi. There was partial agreement which worked for a while and then fell apart. There is a Swahili saying that when elephants fight it is the grass that gets trampled on. It was the ordinary people of Uganda who were suffering under all the changes and the struggle for power.

I went on home leave in the summer of '85. I enjoyed the break even though it was the wettest summer in Ireland for ages. It was just great to be back again. In the home place in Killeenbrack my sister-in-law, Delia, was bravely carrying on with the farm after the death of my brother, Tom. Her two children, Mary and Michael, were growing up fast. Mary was now sitting for her Leaving Cert in Mercy College, Moate. I promised her that after the last exam I would take her and some of her closest classmates for a meal in Athlone to celebrate the occasion. We booked a table in the Prince of Wales hotel. It was very pleasant for me just to sit back and listen to those young ladies bubbling over with excitement, talking of the exams, holiday plans and their future career hopes. The waitress who served us had also been a student in the Mercy school, Moate, and so joined in the general chatter. At one stage she looked at me – I was in civvies – and asked, "Which of these is your daughter?" I smiled and said. "Well actually, all of them call me Father!" There was laughter all round.

The moving statue

Two incidents that summer stand out in my memory. We had the moving statues phenomenon beginning with the statue of Our Lady at Ballinspittle, Co. Cork. It gave rise to many stories and jokes. I learned my own little lesson one wet night when I gave a lift to two hippies outside Mullingar. One asked me what I thought of the happenings at Ballinspittle. I told him that it was all nonsense. "Were you there?" he challenged me. "No," I said. "Then how can you be so sure of yourself?" "Fair point" I told him. "You obviously have an opinion on the matter". He told me he had been there, searching for some meaning to life and had a religious experience which brought him back to the Church. "Good for you," I told him and to myself I said, "Take note of that, wise guy, and keep quiet!" Some time later that year, June Levine, a Jewish lady and a well known journalist with the *Sunday Independent* wrote an interesting article on her experience when she went down to report on the happening. She recounted that as she joined the large crowd at Ballinspittle and fixed her gaze on the statue, the face of Our Lady changed into the face of a Jewish Rabbi. June was amazed and gazed in total wonder. Then her professional instincts took over, told her to get away, walk down the road, clear her head and don't give way to imagination. She did just that, got away from the place and after a considerable time went back and joined the crowd again and looked at the statue. Amazingly she had the same experience. In her article she said that she was simply reporting without comment what she had experienced. Obviously some strange phenomenon was at work.

The adventure of two boys

Another story that summer seems incredible. It concerned two Dublin primary school boys who played truant from school at lunchtime and set off for Dun Laoghaire for a bit of fun. They got on a boat and arrived in Holyhead. They found the railway station and slipped onto the train for London. In Euston they saw a train for Heathrow airport and went aboard. In Heathrow, quietly evading security and customs, they managed to get on a plane heading for New York. Arriving in Kennedy airport, they again managed to get through all controls and inspectors and found themselves in the huge airport car park. This didn't seem like a city so they went up to a policeman and asked him "Hey. Mister, where's New York?" He questioned them gently, took them into an office and gradually the whole story came out. They were given a bit of a tour and put on a plane back to Ireland. I heard the policeman interviewed on radio. He was full of admiration for the boys. "They are what we call streetwise. I predict a great future for them." Apparently the boys had only one trick in the bag which got them through at every checkpoint. They simply said, "Ma is coming with the tickets" and slipped through. Airport officials were most concerned how they could breach security so easily and they wanted to know what airline they had travelled on. The only clue the boys gave them was when they were asked if they had got food on board. "Yes," they said, "They gave us some of that curry stuff". Did this point to Air

India which serves curry as their main meal?   If so, it was all the more shocking, as shortly before, an Air India plane had been blown up off the coast of Ireland and security was supposed to be extremely tight. The last word came from the mother of one of the boys who said, "I wouldn't mind but I told Sheamie not to go too far as his dinner was almost ready". I wonder whatever happened to those two adventurers in later life.

To light a candle

In September I was packing my bags again to return to Uganda. I knew I was going back to a troubled country. One coup had taken place and another seemed imminent. I always asked people to pray for our missionaries especially those working in disturbed areas. I have great faith in the prayers of children. There is a beautiful trust and innocence about how they talk to God. I also think that the prayers of people in hospital or those who are gravely ill are very powerful. One of the last persons I visited before leaving was a close friend, Mary Walsh. She had been chair-person of the co-workers of Mother Teresa of Calcutta. She had been a successful professional woman but was now suffering from lupus. Sometimes it took her over an hour just to get out of bed in the morning. When I gave her a farewell hug and asked her to pray for me she told me, "Every Saturday morning after the nine o'clock Mass in the parish church I light a candle before the statue of Our Lady for your safety." I was very touched by this simple faith-filled gesture. I said goodbye to her and to all my family and friends and was back in Uganda before the end of September.

Chapter 19
The storm breaks

Towards the end of 1985, Uganda was a country in deep political turmoil. It was obvious that the threat to the government from the west was growing with Museveni's army moving steadily towards the capital, Kampala, with little resistance. The reaction of the government in power was simply to enlist more raw recruits from their own tribal ranks and import more arms. It was a tough time for missionaries who carried on their work as best they could. There were road blocks everywhere and small pockets of rebels operated freely. The Christmas period was a very tense time. I helped out in a parish up country with the Christmas Masses and in two locations we had to send a local scout ahead of us just to see if it was safe to go ahead. We got by safely, celebrated the Feast and prayed to the Prince of Peace for our beloved Uganda.

In January we knew that a coup was immanent. I was based in Tororo in the south of the country near the Kenya border. I was due to go to Pallisa, where I had spent my first Christmas after my return to Uganda. I had been asked to give a retreat to the community of Sisters there. Pallisa is over sixty miles north of Tororo, with the town of Mbale in between. Mbale is the capital of the eastern region. We knew something was about to happen as the army had hijacked trucks and buses around Tororo and packed them with armed soldiers. As I headed north for Pallisa on Monday 20th January I met a huge military convoy heading for Kampala. They hogged the middle of the road, lights flashing, soldiers bristling with weapons of all descriptions in a mighty display of arrogance and aggressive power. I reached Pallisa safely. There were about twenty five

Sisters in all including novices and postulants. They ran a school and an orphanage. We began the retreat that evening. It was due to end on Saturday morning. All during the week we were preoccupied with the dread of what might happen. I followed the course of the war on the B.B.C. overseas service as all local communications were cut. By Friday it was obvious that the National Resistance Army led by Museveni was about to take Kampala. It fell on the Saturday without the expected strong resistance. Museveni had deployed his troops well and used some of his boy soldiers in a very clever tactic. In the days leading up to the final assault, he sent them into the city dressed as beggars and ragamuffins. At night they returned and gave detailed reports of the positioning of the Uganda army units. On the morning of the attack he sent them in again in their disguise but this time armed with hand grenades and small bombs. They climbed trees and buildings near army personnel carriers and at the first sign of the assault they flung their grenades right left and centre to create total panic. Museveni led the frontal assault and took control of the capital with relative ease.

Saturday 25th January 1986 is a day I'll long remember. I had heard on the B.B.C. how Kampala had fallen and I thought of all those defeated, retreating, angry, looting soldiers fleeing north to their tribal homelands. Our location was directly in their path although the convent and mission station were thankfully a few hundred yards off the main road. I went into the trading centre. The police station was empty. All ten policemen had fled. The local market, normally crowded, was deserted. The few little shops were being boarded up. The local residents were gathering up children, chickens, goats, bicycles, bits of moveable property and heading for the protection of the bush and the high grass. Fear was on every face and with good reason. Already deserters from the fighting in Kampala were beginning to arrive. Around noon four truckloads of soldiers came with their guns. They smashed open the local petrol station to get fuel for their journey north. They grabbed bicycles and any items of value from any poor unfortunate individual not fast enough to get away and terrified the local population. Some time later there was the sound of gunfire. It was hard to tell what happened. A car arrived with more soldiers. A row broke out and the shooting started. There were four or five deaths. The following day two corpses were still lying on the street. The gunfire was all that was necessary to spread complete panic all round. Grown men, mothers with babies, young children, all alike were caught up in a mad scramble to get away as far as possible from those soldiers.

At the nearby mission and convent we really didn't know what to do. What could one do? Two boys rushed by to say the deserting soldiers were all over the place, looting and terrorising and that some of them were heading our way. They would be here within minutes. I put my car in a shed and put a lock of dubious quality on the door. A good kick would have broken both lock and door. I returned to the large common room where most of the Sisters were assembled. Some wanted to flee into the high grass. I advised against it and said that if the soldiers did invade, we would all go into the chapel next door and I would speak to the soldiers. We waited. I'll never forget that feeling of helplessness and fear in the pit of one's stomach. Little Mary Asio, a girl of six, rushed in and cried out, "Father, give me poison, I don't want to be shot again." I knew Mary's story. Three years before she had seen both parents shot by soldiers. "No, Mary" I said, "Come over here. I'll protect you," and I put a protective arm around her. Big brave me and my tummy in a knot! At one stage I looked at the clock on the wall. It was now afternoon and the clock read 12.30. Uganda is three hours ahead of G.M.T. which meant it was 9.30 a.m. in a Dublin church. I said a fervent prayer that my candle was burning there before the statue of our Blessed Mother. It was.

We braced ourselves for the worst but thank God it didn't come. The bulk of the soldiers took another route out of Pallisa, heading for Soroti further north. Some came our way but they looked a sorry sight, tired, hungry, disillusioned, many of them walking. They still carried guns and so were dangerous. They did some looting. Such is the fear engendered over the years in this unfortunate country that the sight of one army man with a gun is enough to spread panic among the people. The uncertainty and fear persisted throughout the week. All sorts of rumours spread but by and large things were quiet enough. At night sleep didn't come easily and one woke up at the slightest sound. We prayed a lot, Mass, Holy Hours, Rosaries. These were a great source of strength and consolation as also was the knowledge that many were praying for our safety. Some of the psalms and other passages of sacred scripture took on a deeper meaning. There was much fear of what tomorrow would bring so I read out the quote from St. Matthew's gospel where Jesus tells his disciples: *Don't worry about tomorrow; tomorrow will take care of itself. Each day has enough trouble of its own.*

On 31st January, Yoweri Museveni was sworn in as President of Uganda. He promised to restore law and order and human rights and to stamp out corruption and there were high hopes that this time there would be a genuine change. It was badly needed. After years of misrule under Amin and Obote and under the recent regime of Okello, the country had well-nigh collapsed. The old army which was called the Uganda National Liberation Army U.N.L.A. became known cynically as the Uganda National Looting army. With little training, poor morale and leadership, the gun was their license to steal and pillage as they strutted around every town in the country, the officers often the worse offenders. Museveni promised to remedy all this and somehow I had a certain confidence in him. Reports of his army seemed to indicate that they were well disciplined. Are we on the right road at last? His first objective was to extend his control over the vast north-eastern region, disarm the thousands of deserters and eliminate the roving bands of armed robbers that were operating in many areas. Rumours of death and destruction spread widely and we were all very concerned about the welfare of our many colleagues especially those caught up in troubled areas. My own immediate concern was to get back to

Tororo but I wondered if it was safe to travel?

On Monday 3rd February, I heard on the B.B.C. – my only real contact with the outside world – that Mbale had been liberated by Museveni's troops. Okello's fleeing soldiers had wreaked devastation on the town, killing over a hundred people, some prominent citizens and even patients in the hospital. Bishop Odongo, the Catholic bishop who lived in Mbale had his house looted. Mbale College was also looted and one teacher killed.

A few days later I saw some public transport on the road and decided it was safe to travel back to Tororo. I was pleasantly surprised to find no road blocks and friendly young soldiers in evidence in a few places. I called to see Bishop Odongo and he told me of his horrendous experience as gangs looted his house on three occasions and threatened to kill him. We said a prayer of thanksgiving together that we had come through safely and we prayed for our colleagues in Soroti and places north who must still be in the danger zone. I reached Tororo that evening and there was great rejoicing as some rumours had spread that as I hadn't been seen for almost three weeks I must be dead. "Well survived" was the greeting all round. It was like a mini-resurrection. Many of my friends had some exciting tales of their own survival. As I entered my house I saw three bullet holes in the door and a few more on the wall. I left them there for a long time as a grim reminder of what people had been through. That evening we were very relieved to get word from Kampala that our missionary people based there were safe. A week later we heard that our colleagues in Soroti diocese were also safe.

Museveni's troops pushed north and within weeks the whole of Uganda was under their control, in so far as that was possible. Sadly many of the fleeing army from the previous regime kept their guns and often sold them to the local population. Bands of rebels were formed in many places and did a lot of plundering and looting at night. One such group was led by a woman witchdoctor called Alice Lakwena. It's strange what influence witchcraft and superstitious beliefs can have on some people. She marched her motley gang south and the local population were scared stiff. One of my workmen told me in all seriousness that she had smeared her troops with oil which had the power of stopping bullets and turning them back of the ones who fired them. Eventually her gang met up with some disciplined soldiers who killed some of her men and put the rest to flight. A year later another very sinister group assembled under one Joseph Kony. They called themselves the Lord's Resistance Army (L.R.A.) stating they wanted to establish a government based on the Bible. They were the most evil, brutal and treacherous soldiers imaginable. They overran schools and kidnapped young boys and girls. The girls became sex slaves. The boys were forced to join the army and as a way of 'blooding' them, some were ordered to kill their parents. They operated in the north especially along the border with Sudan and they had a ready supply of deadly weapons. They often came south to do their evil work. They continued for years and it is a mark against the new government in Kampala that it failed to deal with them. Under Museveni's new regime the south of the country was peaceful. Much progress was made and conditions in general improved. Goods became available and small shops opened. It was reasonably safe to travel. Some of our mission projects which had been put on hold could now go ahead and we had hopes for future improvement.

Chapter 20
Tales from the front line

The source of the Nile

Winston Churchill who visited Uganda back in 1907 described the country as the pearl of Africa. He was impressed not only by its natural beauty but also by its fertility. Uganda is a beautiful country. To the east there is Mt. Elgon rising to 14,000 feet. To the West there are the rugged Ruwenzori mountains, home to the rare mountain gorilla. To the south we have the vast Lake Victoria – it could contain the whole of Ireland – out of which flows the lordly Nile river on its majestic run through Uganda, Sudan and Egypt. For centuries it was a great challenge to find the source of this great river which flowed into the Mediterranean out of the heart of Africa. It is said that Caesar once sent one of his legions up river to find the source. They never came back, presumably lost in the vast swamps. However there is a theory that they did find their way up the east coast to what is now Tanzania, intermarried with the local women and that is the origin of the Masai tribe. The theory is quite plausible. The faces of the Masai have distinct European features. They have the reputation of being a very warlike tribe. Often young warriors had to prove themselves by killing a lion in single combat, armed with just a spear. They wear a long cloak over their left shoulder in the manner of the Roman toga. In battle, they lock their shields into a phalanx after the manner of the Roman legions. These are telling signs to support the theory.

Explorers such as Burton and Speke were very much engaged in trying to find the source of the Nile. Eventually in July 1862, Speke claimed he had found it as he saw the huge river flow out of the Lake Victoria, near what is now the town of Jinja. He returned to

Britain to be feted, wined and dined for a short period till Burton returned to challenge him. Burton claimed that what Speke discovered was the source of the Congo river and not the Nile. Burton was a much more flamboyant character and many believed him. A big debate was arranged for Newcastle to hear the arguments. On the eve of the debate Speke was crossing a style on his farm with a loaded gun and shot himself. His friends claimed it was an accident. Others questioned how could an experienced hunter and explorer be so careless. He must have been afraid to face Burton. History proved that Speke was right and for a long time a big sign marked the spot where the Nile begins its long journey. The source of the Nile is a favourite place to take visitors and as I lived nearby I saw many celebrities pass my gate from Princess Anne to Colonel Gaddafi. The latter had about two dozen outriders to escort him as he rode by with an air of triumphant haughtiness. How the mighty have fallen.

Fr. Michael Ortner

The southern half of Uganda is very fertile and with proper management could easily produce enough food for the whole country. The northern half has wide tracts of barren territory and the local people often go hungry. One of our priests, Fr. Michael Ortner, was in charge of a parish in the area. Many of his people were in dire need. As so often they turned to him for help and at one stage he was feeding up to five hundred people a day. To buy enough food to meet such needs one has to have a good supply of money. He would collect it from a colleague who in turn would collect it from a foreign exchange bureau in Kampala. The highest printed note in Uganda currency at the time was a one hundred shilling note, value about one dollar. To collect a large sum of Uganda currency one needed a large bag, suitcase or cardboard box.

To follow this story, know that a million Uganda shillings equals roughly a thousand dollars. One day Fr. Michael collected ten million shillings in a large box and placed it safely in a room in his house. The next day the box was gone; it was obviously an inside job. Fr. Michael was now in a dilemma. Apart from his great loss, he was reluctant to call the local police as he didn't want to reveal that he kept large sums in his house. So he let it go and did what he could with the little money he had. A week later the thieves felt he must have collected more money and this time they struck openly.

Michael had a generator to supply light and power for the house. It was housed in a cement hut some distance from the mission house. Late at night Michael went over to switch off the engine. As he did so there was a noise. Michael turned round to see the shadow of a man in the small doorway. He had a gun in his hand and demanded the keys of the mission house and the safe. Pent up anger overtook Michael and with a roar he hurled the spanner at the gunman who dived back. Michael crouched in the corner of the cement hut till he saw the barrel of the gun being shoved inside and the gun went off, the bullet hitting the floor in front of Michael's foot. Michael charged out making a swipe at the gunman as he did so. He raced for the house with the gunman after him. Unfortunately he tripped and fell. The gunman fired point blank down on him. Michael passed out. The gunman grabbed the keys from his pocket and with two or three other robbers quickly ransacked the house, grabbed what little money they could find and loaded a few items of some value into an old car and drove quickly away knowing the gunfire would have attracted attention.

When the coast was clear people came from nearby houses. Michael's curate, an African priest, with some help, managed to raise Michael up, laid him on a mattress in the back of a pick-up and drove him to the nearest mission hospital some fifteen miles away at Kamuli. Here good fortune was with him. A young Dutch volunteer doctor had arrived just the week before. He was a skilled surgeon and in a makeshift theatre in the dead of night he worked on Michael and saved his life. Miraculously the bullet had gone right through his body without fatal consequences. As he was being prepared for the operation Michael was semi-conscious and was muttering continuously. Thinking he wanted to make his confession the priest leaned forward to catch his words. What Michael was saying in broken German (he is from the Tyrol) was not any confession of sins but: "The fools, the fools, little did they know that tomorrow I was going to collect more money!" He made a good recovery and returned to work in his parish. Another touch of black humour emerged. From the bullet holes in his T shirt it seemed he must have been shot from the front while Michael claimed he had pitched forward on his face and he was shot in the back. The mystery was solved by claiming Michael must have been wearing his T shirt back to front!

Meanwhile the local police went to work and flushed out the usual suspects. One fellow was caught in his hut with a box of money. Two policemen dragged him outside and started to beat the daylights out of him. They then displayed a box with a million shillings in it. This raised a question. Fr. Michael had said they stole a small sum of money so where did all this extra money come from? He then had to tell them about the ten million stolen the previous week. The thief having been beaten badly appealed to Fr. Michael for help. He told Fr. Michael that there was at least two million in the box in his house and he saw the police stealing the other million. Word of the ten million stolen aroused feverish interest. The district police were called in. They beat up the local police demanding all the money already recovered and there was a mad search for the rest. Suspects were found and beaten. Fr. Michael pleaded at least for the return of the two million. "Oh no," he was told, "This must be kept as exhibit for the trial." Michael knew he was on a loser. He never saw any of the money again. He cut back on the help he was giving and thanked God he was still alive. The following July he celebrated the Golden Jubilee of his ordination. The parish put on a great feast for the occasion. There were many speeches praising his great ministry and all the help he gave to his people and there were many tokens of appreciation. I spoke at the end and added my own words of praise but referring to the events of the past I reminded them of how much he suffered on their behalf, that the money was never recovered and that there must be many in the congregation who knew who the thieves were. Let them all examine their own consciences.

Bishop Willigers

Bishop Joseph Willigers from the Netherlands was my classmate and close friend. In 1967 he was appointed Bishop of the newly established diocese of Jinja. He reluctantly accepted the position saying that this new post should have been given to an African priest. At that stage he was the only white face among 18 Bishops in Uganda. He sometimes jokingly referred to himself as the black sheep of the family! At the time of his appointment little did he know of the turmoil that lay ahead with the coming of Idi Amin to power, the expulsion of all the Asian traders and the general lawlessness. Through it all the Bishop continued his pastoral work, visiting parishes, administering confirmations and supporting his people in many ways. Even a double heart bypass operation didn't slow him down. He had three cars taken from him at gunpoint. His house was attacked more than once and there were bullet holes through his back door as a grim reminder. He never lost his sense of humour and there was always a great welcome for any visitor in his modest house on Rubaga Hill.

After Museveni took over the country things calmed down a bit and the situation in Jinja was reasonably peaceful. On New Year's day, 1990, I called to wish him a happy New Year and he told me what had happened the night before. He was alone in the house, having a light supper when in walked two men, one carrying a gun. "We want the deck; hand over the deck," one shouted. The Bishop hadn't a clue what they were demanding. Not having a television set he didn't know the term video-deck. "I haven't got any deck", he told them. "Yes, you have, hand it over". The Bishop's house is a rectangular building with rooms built around a grassy rectangle. There were lights on in a big room across the way showing cardboard boxes and other items. It was the diocesan office. The robber shouted, "It must be in that room, take us there". Joe, still not knowing what they were looking for, took them across. They started ripping open various boxes. Most of them contained altar breads and linen. "It's not here" one shouted. He was getting very impatient. Suddenly the Bishop realised he was standing beside the diocesan safe with a sizeable amount of money inside and he had the keys in his pocket, with a witless criminal pointing a gun at him. Before the penny might drop Joe shouted, "It must be in the sitting room; come, I'll show you." He led them across to the sitting room next to his own bedroom. There was a large radio and hi-fi system on a side table. "There it is," he shouted and while they were distracted he dived into his bedroom and locked the door. The thieves grabbed what they could and left. It was only when Fr. Emmanuel, his secretary, returned later and Joe asked what the thieves were looking for, he was told what a deck was. "But I don't have a TV so how could I have a deck?" he asked. "But I have one," said Emmanuel, "I was presented with one yesterday. The thieves must have known." "Well, for God's sake get rid of it" said the Bishop.

Bishop Joseph Willigers whose original intention was to serve for just five years before handing over actually served as Bishop of Jinja for over thirty five years. In 1992 he celebrated the Silver Jubilee of his Episcopal ordination which was also the Silver Jubilee of the diocese of Jinja. I was one of many who helped to organise the event. It was a wonderful occasion. A huge congregation attended to pay their respects. Almost every Bishop in Uganda came to pay tribute to a wonderful missionary bishop who served the people of Uganda so faithfully in good times and in bad. Even after he retired as Bishop he continued to serve the local church. Ill health forced him to return to Holland in 2012 and he died peacefully in September of that year just short of his 82nd birthday.

Chapter 21
The inimitable Fr. John

Fr. John Neidegger was a priest who worked beside me in Tororo diocese. He was a German diocesan priest who joined the Benedictine Order and came out to Uganda with the intention of setting up a Benedictine monastery. There was already a community of Benedictine Sisters established. For someone who joined a contemplative community Fr. John was one of the most active and remarkable men I ever met. He applied to the town council of Tororo to buy a large tract of land near the town as a site for his new monastery. It was occupied mostly by squatters and the local Mafia criminals. The town council were happy to let Fr. John have the land hoping to see some good development there. The Mafia were willing to move further out as they viewed the development as a new source for their looting activities. Fr. John was happy to have a sizeable area to develop and in which to build his monastery. He was an outstanding organiser. Over a few years he developed a farm, built a garage and gave plenty of employment to local workmen. He imported containers of used clothes which he sold at a low price to finance the building of his monastery. Rather than one large building, he had designed a spacious central building and then a series of well-constructed round huts after the style of the traditional African compound. Each student/candidate would have his own private accommodation and share a common chapel, dining room, library and recreation room. The layout was well planned and within a short period a number of aspiring candidates joined. Fr. John arranged that some of them would continue their studies at a Seminary in Nairobi. He acquired the services of Fr. Aelred, a

Benedictine monk from Belmont, Herefordshire, to serve as Novice Master. All seemed to be going very well.

Any signs of prosperity attract thieves. One well known robber, a violent character, did a lot of damage and Fr. John had the police remove him. He vowed vengeance. Fr. John had helped so many people that they would warn him of danger. One early morning a boy came and told him that the man had come back and was armed and was in a certain hut. John called the police who promised to take action. When challenged, the thief came out shooting and the police gunned him down. Of course he had friends among the mafia and they planned their next move. Fr. John was duly warned that the monastery would be attacked on the night of October 9th. That is a significant date in Uganda as it marks Independence Day. Fr. John appealed to the police and army for protection but as the robbers had rightly surmised, everybody would be too busy celebrating that night. The criminals thought they would have an easy ride but they had reckoned without Fr. John. Although his only defence was two air guns he planned his strategy. He procured a couple of tin hats, dressed two of his workmen in make-believe uniforms, put them in the back of his car with the barrels of the air-guns just visible through the windows. He then drove into enemy territory and called aside an old man and gave him this message. "You know the criminals who are doing such damage here and all over. I happen to know that tonight they are planning to attack the monastery but we are ready for them. We are planning an ambush and we intend to wipe them out. Don't tell anybody, do you understand? Don't tell anybody or our plan will fail." John knew that this was one instruction that would not be observed and word spread quickly. John drove away at speed. The Mafia quickly changed their plans. That night they crossed over the border to Kenya where they looted a village and killed an old man. On the way back they encountered the Kenya police who shot three of them dead.

John was extremely generous to people but also did some foolish things with the best of intentions such as giving large sums of money to people who promised to pay it back. We missionaries had a principle: give money as a donation or don't give it. With the conditions in Uganda, expecting people to pay it back was one way of losing friends. John once funded a local farmer to buy a tractor. The farmer could use it for himself and for hire but he had to pay a small percentage of his earnings to Fr. John and park the tractor at the monastery every weekend to show who owned it. That worked all right for two or three weekends and then the farmer declared that he owned the tractor. When the police took possession of it for Fr. John, the man was laughed at and vowed vengeance. People who knew him warned Fr. John. The danger was real. On one occasion when I called to see John I saw a strange looking man at the gate. He eyed me up and down carefully as I passed in. John was not at home. The following day John asked me if I had noticed the man at the gate. I said yes. He told me he was a known hit-man sent to kill him. One of the workmen recognised him and sent for the police. They arrested him and found he was carrying a loaded pistol and confessed to his mission. I then remembered how he had carefully eyed me. As I was sometimes mistaken by strangers for Fr. John I mentioned wryly that if I'm ever bumped off, I would like to die under my own name!

Little did Fr. John know that an enemy lurked within the monastery itself. A student/candidate whom John, for good reasons, did not promote for further studies kept a deep grudge within himself and bided his time. The student was from the west of Uganda where many of the army stationed in Tororo were from. One morning a group of five army men arrived and demanded to see Fr. John. They told him, "We have good information that you have weapons hidden in the monastery grounds and we have come to search" Without further ado two of them went to a tree behind the building, started digging and unearthed a number of rifles. It was so obvious that they knew where to dig and that the guns had been planted. Fr. John protested his innocence. He was taken away and locked in a police cell in town. As soon as I heard the news I contacted the Bishop and the German ambassador. I visited John in his cell, saw the policeman in charge who agreed with me that it was all an evil plot against John. John knew immediately who had done it, the student who had easy access to friends in the army. The said student waited till late that day, packed his few belongings and left the monastery for good. He returned to his people in western Uganda and the following year was killed in the fighting near the Rwanda border. When the news broke a notice was put up in the monastery by Fr. Aelred asking for prayers for the repose of his soul and kindly adding a quote in Latin *De mortuis nihil nisi bonum dicitur* (Speak only good of the dead).

John was well treated while in custody. When I asked about his release, they told me they were subject to the army and so could do nothing but assured me that he would be released soon. The army had other ideas. They knew John had access to money and they were determined to extract a big price for his release. He was taken under guard to Kampala and kept in an army cell. We informed Cardinal Nsubuga who went to President Museveni to plead his case. John was released into the care of the Cardinal and eventually allowed to come back to Tororo but the charge was held over him for more than a year before it was finally dropped. No money was paid.

John continued to attract attention and another episode had a tragic ending. John knowing the danger he was in often slept in a different monastery hut each night. Late one night gunmen came for him. They roused a student up and demanded that he take them to where John was. It's not known whether the student knew or not. When the gunmen failed to get the information they murdered him. It happened on the night of 25th August, 1990. He was Bro. Denis Robert Wandega, a novice member of the Benedictine community. He was buried with full honours and on his headstone is the inscription: *"A Martyr for Christ"*.

It was time for a real assessment of the future of the monastery. It was established under the overall authority of St. Ottilien

Monastery in Germany and the Abbot of that monastery came to Tororo to decide the future. He discussed the whole situation with Bishop Odongo and many others including myself. There was talk of closure. There were obviously too many activities in the vicinity. Fr. John agreed to hand over the running of the farm and the garage and the contents of a number of containers to the local diocese. Another priest came out from Germany to help. In the end it was decided that it would be better if Fr. John left. He reluctantly said goodbye and left for another African country. He wrote me a farewell letter thanking me for my friendship and support. He was one of the most remarkable men I ever met. The monastery he founded continues to attract candidates and is doing well.

Chapter 22
Mission Candidates

In the early days when our missionaries were given a territory to evangelise, their first responsibility was to establish the Church, preach the Gospel and try to attract converts. They did this very successfully and soon churches and schools were built. The mission compound became the centre of much activity meeting the various spiritual and temporal needs of the people. The Sunday Mass became a great social occasion. Many people brought their children for baptism; many adults offered themselves for instruction. Over the years, some young men expressed the wish to become priests. Seminaries were established to train them. The long-term aim was to replace the missionaries with local clergy. This was happening in many places. The increase in local vocations compensated for the decline in missionary personnel. In Uganda in the nineteen sixties the National Seminary near Kampala had over one hundred students preparing for the priesthood. This was seen as great progress. Then it emerged that some individuals asked about the possibility of joining our missionary Society rather than the local diocese. From the beginning Rome had not allowed us to accept them. Our job was to build up the local church and all vocations should be channelled in that direction. Now there was a change in this policy. The local church had become sufficiently strong in itself to become missionary. Pope Paul V1 made a ground-breaking plea that the African church should now reach out to others in sharing the good news of the Gospel. Who better to help them do so than a missionary society like our own? Whether we should accept candidates from our mission territories into our Society became the question of the day. There were arguments for and against. Was it advisable to accept candidates from a foreign culture into what was an essentially European Society? Would it not be better to establish an African missionary Institute? The question would have to be decided by the delegates at the forthcoming General Chapter of the Society. The Chapter meets every six years with representatives from all the countries where we work. Its purpose is to assess our mission work, to plan ahead and to decide on various issues which arise. The next Chapter was due to meet at MHM headquarters in London, in July 1988.

In 1987 I was elected Society Superior of our missionaries in Uganda. There were more than fifty of us working in four different dioceses and it was felt that there should be one centre of administration in view of important decisions which lay ahead. My responsibility was to keep contact with headquarters at home and to help co-ordinate the various activities in the different dioceses where we work and of course the welfare of the members. Some were working in very troubled areas. When Museveni took control there were high hopes of peace and stability and in the south of the country a fair measure of success was achieved. In the north-eastern regions large areas of the countryside were in rebel hands. Different groups operated. Some were gangs of rebels composed of soldiers from previous regimes and some were just criminal gangs cashing in on the disturbed state of the country. Mission stations were attacked. The big mission hospital near Lira, run by the Verona Sisters, was looted. Over two hundred patients, many of them lepers, had to flee and some were killed. After every raid the missionaries as always did what they could to help. It was a very challenging time.

Morale among our missionaries remained high. No one asked to leave. At our occasional get-togethers hair-raising stories were exchanged and narrow escapes related. Underneath it all was a feeling that this was where the missionary should be, serving the people in time of greatest need. The practical help they were able to give was substantial. When the Karimajong warriors raided Teso country and stole all their cattle and the children there had no milk, Fr. Phelan, through his brother, Paddy, was able to import by air, bags of powdered milk in the short term and a whole container of it in the long term and thus save countless lives. I witnessed Ko Klaver, one of our Associate members, more than once leave in the early morning with a pick-up loaded with blankets and medicines. He was responding to an appeal from a distant mission station which had just been looted. Such journeys were not without considerable risk. Although most sides respected the missionaries, everyone was a potential target. The rebels once fired a grenade at Klaver's pick-up which thankfully missed. On his return journey he was stopped by the gang who apologised for the attack!

At the end of 1987 I was elected as delegate to represent Uganda at the forthcoming General Chapter. We had many meetings of our men in Uganda to discuss our problems, what the priorities of our Society should be and how best we could further the work of evangelisation. I looked forward to coming home for the Chapter, meeting fellow delegates and sharing our stories. I intended combining my travelling home for the Chapter with a short vacation in Ireland. While returning to Ireland was usually a joyful experience for me, it was sometimes tinged with sorrow as when I returned for my brother Tom's death in '83. Sadly his wife, Delia, died just four years later in May 1987. It happened suddenly one Sunday night shortly after retiring when she had a massive brain haemorrhage. Her son Michael was the only one in the house with her. The young lad rushed to the neighbours for help but Delia died shortly afterwards. It was a terrible blow to her children Michael and Mary and to all. At the time, I was up country in Uganda out of reach of communication and it was almost a week later before I heard the tragic news. I was totally shattered and my first thoughts were for Mary and Michael and how they could cope with such a tragedy. I wished I could have been with them. On my return I was very relieved to see how well they had come through their great ordeal.

The General Chapter debated at length the question of accepting mission candidates into our Society. The decision to accept them was passed almost unanimously and the members looked forward to welcoming African, Indian and Philippino candidates into our Society. Houses of formation to help them prepare to become Mill Hill missionaries would have to be established in different countries. I was commissioned to establish one in Uganda. I flew out from Heathrow to Nairobi on 22nd October, on my way back to Uganda, with packed luggage and looking forward to the work ahead, but sadly, another tragedy had occurred.

Chapter 23
The ultimate price

On Sunday evening, 23rd October, I was relaxing in our house in Nairobi, planning to spend a day or two shopping before returning to Uganda. Then word came through that one of our priests in Uganda, Fr. Kees Spil, had been murdered by robbers the night before. It was tragic news which stunned us all. The funeral was the following day and although I was some three hundred miles away I knew I had to be present.

Fr. Kees was Dutch, a relatively young, hard-working missionary who was parish priest of Buswale, a country district in Jinja diocese. He had been shopping in Jinja town on the Saturday and called to see some of his missionary colleagues that evening before returning to his mission station some thirty miles away. His friend, Fr. Groenewoud tried to persuade him to stay the night, but no, he had a busy Sunday planned for the morrow. He reached home with two African helpers, tired and glad to be back. They decided to sit outside and have a beer. They had scarcely sat down when three armed men appeared out of the shrubbery nearby and without warning one of them fired straight at Fr. Spil. Badly wounded he pitched forward in agony. His two companions fled. One gunman stood guard over the wounded man who was calling out for help. The other two started looting the house, gathering up any valuables that could be easily carried away. After some time they emerged with bags of loot. They called to the gunman guarding Fr. Spil who was still crying out. Before going away the gunman fired again at Fr. Spil, killing him outright. Then they all fled.

Shocked neighbours all gathered around to mourn and to carry their dead priest into the house. The police were sent for. The Bishop and other priests were called but there was little anyone could do. Robberies were common enough but this was a brutal killing. Questions were asked. Did Fr. Kees know his attackers? Had he once dismissed dishonest workers who kept a grievance against him? Nobody knew. The tragedy was felt by all. Fr. Kees had been a dedicated priest working to develop the parish and was in the process of building a large community hall for the people.

Funerals cannot be postponed long in the tropics and when I got the tragic news and the time of the funeral, midday on Monday, I immediately packed my few belongings, borrowed a car from a colleague and set out on the long journey. I made an overnight stop at our house in Kisumu and continued to Uganda on Monday morning. I left early making allowance for possible delays at the border crossing and I reached Buswale parish church just in time. A large crowd had gathered for the funeral. It was a very sad occasion. There was great mourning at the death of a very good priest. Members of his family had managed to come out from Holland. Some of his missionary colleagues wept openly. Bishop Willigers led the Mass and preached. I paid my own tribute at the end. We were all so shocked at the mindless act of murder. After the burial I looked through the house. One of the saddest sights was to see the bloodstained and bullet-riddled clothes of Fr. Kees in the corner of his bedroom. The robbers were never caught although some months later two thieves were caught near Jinja and the police claimed that these were the ones responsible for Fr. Spil's murder. They were lynched by an angry mob.

The murder of Fr. Spil was the latest of the tragic deaths in the history of our missionaries in Uganda. Sadly it would not be the last. Previous tragic events included the murder of Fr. John Tauber. In July of 1979, after the fall of Amin, Fr. John, from Tyrol who was parish priest of Amuria in the north of Uganda was alerted one evening by three young men, two in civilian clothes, one in a military uniform. They had a story about an accident and an injured man who needed help. Fr. Tauber who was suspicious of their motives yet was anxious in case some one really needed him. He set out in his pick-up and took some school boys with him. Two kilometres from the mission the soldier ordered him to stop. He fired in the air and told everyone to run. He demanded the keys of the pick-up. Fr. Tauber refused and tried to resist. He was shot dead, dumped by the roadside and the soldier and the other two stole the car and drove away. Fr. John's body was taken to the mission and buried in his own parish where he had given twelve years of dedicated service.

Some nine months later on the night of 24th April, 1980, robbers attacked Mbale College. There was a small farm attached to the college and some animals had been sold that day and the thieves were after the money. They were spotted before they could gain entrance and someone slammed the door shut. The angry criminals just sprayed the building with bullets. Sadly, one of our priests, Fr. McGrath from Birmingham who was inside was fatally wounded. The gunfire attracted attention and the thieves ran away. Fr. McGrath was rushed to hospital but died shortly after arrival. He had served the diocese for many years, was widely respected and had a great sense of humour. He was a teacher and acted as bursar for the college. One of his last messages said with wry humour was, "I'm sorry, the books are in a bit of a mess". Three other missionaries were wounded in the attack but thankfully recovered.

The most recent murder was that of a young Irish priest from Headford, Co. Galway, Fr. Declan O'Toole. It happened on 21st March, 2002. After his ordination in 1997, Fr. Declan was appointed to Uganda. He was assigned to Karamoja, a very primitive area in northern Uganda inhabited by a warlike nomadic tribe, the Karimajong. They used to hunt with spears but in recent times they were able to get plenty of guns from soldiers fleeing after defeat in various coups. The government rightly wanted to disarm them. With a tribe that had little respect for authority this would require great tact and diplomacy. An aggressive approach would be fiercely resisted. Our missionaries there were highly respected for what they were doing for the people and they had some influence in persuading the warriors to give up their weapons. The army played rough and ill treated some people. At one stage Fr. Declan protested at their tactics which were counter productive. For his efforts, he got roughed up himself by some army men. Fr. Declan withdrew for some time. Word of the incident was sent to the Irish ambassador who complained to President Museveni. Obviously some knuckles were rapped. It's difficult to know what really happened. When Fr. Declan returned to his mission he was a marked man. One day driving from his mission in a pick-up vehicle with his African cook and a mission helper, he was stopped by two soldiers. Without warning the soldiers opened fire and Fr. Declan and his two companion were ruthlessly murdered. Nothing was taken from the vehicle. The bodies were brought back to the mission and word spread of the dreadful atrocity. Shock was everywhere. The people all gathered to mourn the deaths and they wanted their beloved young priest to be buried among them. However, after a solemn funeral ceremony for the three dead men Fr. Declan's body was taken back to Ireland and buried in the family plot in Headford. He was just thirty one years of age, a young priest, full of enthusiasm and Gospel dedication. The two soldiers who committed the murders were later arrested, tried and executed. However there was a strong suspicion that they were mere stooges acting on orders from above.

Fr. Declan's parents and family were obviously distraught by the tragic events as were all the parishioners and neighbours back home as he was very popular and was always involved in local affairs and in sports, especially the GAA. However, with true Christian discernment, the family could distinguish between the ordinary people that Fr. Declan served in Uganda and the criminals who carried out the murder. They continued to collect money to support the projects Declan had been involved in. Then four years later a beautiful event took place which cast a different light on the district and the people that Fr. Declan served.

Fr. Declan's sister, Ita O'Toole, a social worker, was engaged to be married. She had visited her brother in Karamoja a couple of times and was captivated by the wild primitive conditions and the rugged beauty of the area, so different from the relative opulence of her home country. Together with her fiancé, Tim O'Connor, a civil engineer, they decided to have their wedding in Uganda, in the very parish where Fr. Declan had served so well. Ita recalls, "I did it purely for the memory of Declan. It was a great tribute to him and to the people of Karamoja whom he cared so much about and gave his life for."

The two families and some friends took themselves off to Uganda for the wedding and headed to the north of the country, to Kotido, where Ita and Tim were married on 1st October, 2005, the first Catholic wedding in the mission Fr. Declan had helped to develop. All the visitors were overwhelmed by the welcome they received. The parish choir and dancers put a huge effort into organising the celebration. In the African culture, Mass is a celebration of joy and the wedding Mass was something very special. Afterwards Ita and Tim were initiated into the Karimajong culture, dressed in animal skins and presented with many gifts including a goat and some chickens. A great feast was had by all. The bridal couple and guests were reluctant to leave but eventually headed for Uganda's capital, Kampala, where Ita and Tim were received by the Irish ambassador. They found an Irish pub where all relaxed with many friends. Ita and Tim then flew on to Zanzibar for their honeymoon and the guests flew home with lasting memories of a great celebration.

Chapter 24
The work must go on

When Yowere Museveni became president in January 1986 he promised to restore security and to eliminate corruption. He achieved limited success in the south of the country. Small businesses opened up and household goods became more available. Coffee and tea plantations were restored and growers got reasonable prices. However extensive areas in the north of the country remained very troubled with rebel gangs operating freely, many of them ex-soldiers from previous regimes. They had easy access to guns and one can reasonably ask why this was so.

At the U.N. and elsewhere during this period there were many demands to check the spread of nuclear weapons. A far bigger problem for Africa was the huge proliferation of small arms, sold to tin-pot dictators by traders in both East and West Even when Idi Amin was expelled from the Commonwealth, one of his planes made a weekly trip to Stanstead airport in London to pick up supplies of arms, booze and surveillance equipment for his army. The gun running continued under the dubious pretext of free trade. After the fall of the dictator many fleeing soldiers grabbed two or three rifles to enable them to loot or to barter them for food and other goods. Some were discarded. Near Tororo hidden in high grass I found an AK47 Russian made rifle with three magazines of live ammunition. I had it in my room for weeks before handing the lot into the local army barracks.

In the north of Uganda extensive areas were in rebel hands. As always the ordinary people suffered most and turned to the missionaries for help. Many came to the mission compound every night for food and shelter. We were able to get some help from abroad, clothes, food and medicines. Fr. Phelan's brother, Paddy, set up an organisation in London called SPICMA (Special Projects in Christian Mission Areas) and was able to send several containers of much needed help from which all poor people benefited, whether they were Christians or not. Other missionaries imported containers of needed supplies. The Catholic mission clinics were often the only lifeline for people wounded or disease ridden.

In spite of the many problems ordinary parish work continued. Large crowds attended Mass and received the sacraments. Schools continued to run and many small projects were started. Catechetical centres were established to train local catechists who played an important part in the running of parishes. Although travelling was sometimes hazardous – I was twice warned of rebel activity on the road ahead – our missionaries had regular get-togethers to discuss mutual concerns and just to support one another. I was always impressed by the overall good-spirit and morale of all our members.

Chapter 25
A new parish

In 1990, Archbishop Wamala asked me if Mill Hill Missionaries would be willing to take over a large area outside Jinja town and develop it as a separate parish. It was a very poor area of several thousand people, many living in slum conditions. They had no permanent church, no school or medical facilities. They didn't even have running water. After due consultation, on behalf of our Society, I accepted responsibility for this new great initiative.

To develop this parish from scratch was a mammoth task and the man chosen for the job was Fr. Len Wiedemayer, a colleague and close friend. He had wide pastoral and teaching experience and proved to be the ideal choice. He set about the undertaking with incredible energy. He had spent years teaching and now many of his former students had positions in local government and he used their influence to provide local amenities including running water. He drew up plans for a church and schools. We got financial help from various sources. On my visits to the United States I always visited my cousin and close friend, Msgr. Shane McGuire. He was pastor of a parish in Sound Beach, Long Island. He had built a beautiful new church and developed a thriving Christian community. When I explained what we were doing in Uganda he insisted that he wanted to help and invited me to preach an appeal in his church at all the Masses one Sunday. The people were extremely generous and I raised over fifteen thousand dollars which was given to help develop our new parish. We got help from other sources too. Within a few years, Fr. Len had built a large church and established three primary schools and one large secondary school and a medical centre. Last on his list was a modest house for himself and his assistant priests. One of these was Fr. Donal Harney from Co. Galway, who was chaplain to the schools and also helped out in parish work. The achievements of Fr. Len within a short time were truly remarkable.

A Health Care programme.

In any such area one of the chief concerns is healthcare. With this in mind, Fr. Len built a convent and invited The Franciscan Missionary Sisters to take up residence and pioneer a programme of healthcare. The task facing them was enormous. People were suffering from a variety of preventable diseases such as malaria, dysentery, typhoid, skin conditions, TB and HIV/AIDS. In many cases the poor health was the result of bad housing, overcrowding, poor sanitation, alcoholism and drug abuse. Unemployment and illiteracy were at a very high level. It was difficult to know where to begin but the Sisters took on the challenge with great courage and resolution.

A community based Health Care programme was considered the best approach. This would involve selling the idea to the people who would then select members from among themselves to be trained as community health workers. They in turn would work with their own communities helping to bring about change through health care education. When the project was slow to start the Sisters realised there was a bigger problem facing them. This emerged when some old women when asked what they needed most simply said, "Please teach us to read and write". So it was seen that an adult literacy programme was a priority. This meant shelving the community based health care programme at least for a while. An Adult Literacy programme was started. A couple of teachers volunteered to help and some books were acquired. It had a slow start because of the shame attached to illiteracy. First a few old women came forward and then more picked up courage. Other problems surfaced. Many of them needed reading glasses. Help was sought in this area and the programme continued and attracted a growing number. It was a great occasion when after a year the first members received certificates of literacy skills. Then the health care programme took off. It began with the training of local health care workers who were very proud to receive their certificates. These then gave great voluntary service educating the community in all matters related to healthy living. The numbers attending the Adult Literacy classes increased and gradually men began to attend as well which required courage on their part to admit their illiteracy. More space was needed for the increased classes. In the dry season, one could put chairs and stools outside under the shade of some big mango trees but this was very much a temporary solution. The programmes had grown and more staff was required. Something would have to be done.

Ireland Aid

The Irish Embassy in Kampala was approached for help and detailed plans were presented to Ireland Aid. A very generous sum was provided to built a large Community Centre and within a year this was up and running. There was great excitement when this was completed as it provided great accommodation for many literacy and healthcare programmes. When President Mary McAleese visited Uganda in 2001, this was one of the parishes she visited and unveiled a plaque acknowledging the generosity of Ireland Aid for this development. In her own inimitable way she greeted the staff individually and praised the work of the missionaries who had initiated the great programme of literacy and healthcare. Fr. Donal Harney was there to greet the President.

The parish was dedicated to St. Charles Lwanga, one of the Uganda martyrs. Its development is just one illustration of the work of our missionaries for the overall good of the people. A new world is opened up for them with opportunities for education and employment. To accommodate the large number of Christians another new church was built later. Being there at the beginning, I was very proud to see the new parish develop so well. I was recalled from Uganda in 1996 but returned on a visit in 2004. I happened to be there on Easter Sunday and the parish priest asked me to lead the Sunday liturgy. The Mass began at 10 o'clock and it was past midday when it finished. It was a wonderful celebration of joy and thanksgiving. In speaking to the huge congregation I reflected on how the parish had developed with strong leadership from the missionaries but it was done by the participation and great co-operation from so many people. It was their parish, their church, their Community Centre. They had a right to celebrate. This was real Resurrection.

Chapter 26
Queen of Apostles Philosophy Centre, Jinja. (P.C.J.)

The decision of the General Chapter of 1988 to accept candidates from our mission countries into our Society was a major development and I was commissioned to initiate the programme in Uganda. It would entail the establishment of formation and academic centres to cater for the candidates who might apply to join our Society. Fortunately other Societies were at the same stage of development and the Superiors of four Congregations came together to plan accordingly. The four Societies involved were the Missionaries of Africa (known as the White Fathers), the Congregation of Holy Cross, the Comboni Missionaries and the Mill Hill Missionaries. These were the founding members of the new Philosophy Centre which would provide common academic training for future candidates for all the Congregations. Each group would have its own centre for the spiritual and moral formation of future members. I was elected chairman of the planning committee and later chairman of the board of governors of the new Philosophy Centre.

We had to start from scratch. Our first task was to find a suitable location. Some wanted the Centre to be in Kampala but I pressed hard for Jinja as Bishop Willigers generously offered twenty five acres of diocesan land on the outskirts of the town as a site for the new Centre and his offer was gratefully accepted. Construction of the new buildings began in September 1991. While these new headquarters were being built the students already accepted were housed in rented quarters. We had the official opening of the

Institute in September 1989.

The whole project required a lot of planning and financing and as chairman of the board I had a few sleepless nights worrying about the many problems. However, funding agencies were quite generous. We were fortunate in choosing good architects and contractors and the project went ahead successfully. The opening Mass in the new headquarters was celebrated on the 24th October, 1992. The buildings were blest by Bishop Willigers in the presence of the Apostolic Nuncio and representatives of all the Congregations involved. The number of students then attending was sixty one.

Over the years the whole project flourished. The Institute continues to fulfil its original purpose, that is, the education of African candidates for the missionary and religious apostolate. Many more Congregations send their students there now and courses are available in a wide range of religious subjects. These courses are open to women also. Mill Hill candidates have come there from Cameroon, Congo, Kenya and Uganda. We now have an increasing number of priests in our Society from these countries. This helps to compensate for the recent lack of candidates from European countries.. It is quite a turnaround. People sometimes ask me if we will one day see African priests coming to re-evangelise Ireland.

In May 2014, as one of the founding members of the Philosophy Centre, I was pleased to receive an invitation to attend its Silver Jubilee celebrations. I was unable to attend but sent my best wishes and heartiest congratulations to all concerned on its great success.

Chapter 27
The Centenary of our Society's arrival in Uganda

The 6th September, 1995, was a special day for our Society in Uganda. A hundred years before on that date the first Mill Hill missionaries arrived. The group consisted of a Bishop and four priests commissioned by Rome to evangelise the territory known as Upper Nile, an area almost twice the size of Ireland, stretching from Kampala in Uganda deep into Western Kenya. The area was totally devoid of any Christian presence. The small band of intrepid missionaries had left Mill Hill, London, on 6th May, 1895. The group consisted of Bishop Hanlon from Manchester, Fr. Prendergast and Fr. Matthews from Scotland, Fr. Kestens from the Netherlands and Fr. Luke Plunkett from Co. Cavan, Ireland.

When they arrived in Mombasa a truly epic journey of over eight hundred miles lay ahead of them to be covered on foot. It is hard for us to imagine the incredible difficulties the journey entailed. They hired some porters to help with the luggage and purchased five donkeys and set off. They followed the old caravan route of traders, much of it through rough bush country, high vegetation, some jungle, swamps and fast flowing rivers. They had to cross the rift valley and negotiate the steep escarpment. Some porters deserted them, often stealing some of their luggage. They ran out of food. They had a close brush with the fierce hostile Nandi tribe who had vowed vengeance on all foreigners because of the deaths of some of their men at the hands of traders. Despite all this they completed their long trek and entered Kampala on the 6th September 1895.

They got a great welcome all round especially from a group of White Fathers who had been working in Uganda since 1879. Bishop

Hanlon and his small group got down to work without delay. They were given a large tract of land by Kabaka (King) Mwanga, in Nsambya, on the outskirts of Kampala, near his own palace. The first small church was erected there in October. A splendid church was built later by our Mill Hill Brothers and now stands on that site. It was the beginning of a great apostolate which saw mission stations established in outlying areas. Many adults came for instruction. Small Christian communities grew up. Children were baptised. Churches and schools were built.

Subsequent groups of Mill Hill men arrived over the following years to further the progress of evangelisation. There followed great expansion which saw parishes set up across Eastern Uganda and into Western Kenya. The year 1903 saw the arrival of the first missionary Sisters from the Abbey School, Mill Hill, London. Bishop Hanlon, home on leave, had asked for volunteers and six Sisters accompanied him back to Uganda. They included a young Sr. Kevin, (Teresa Kearney from Co. Wicklow). She later became known far and wide as Mama Kevina for her outstanding work among the poor. She founded a Congregation of African Sisters which is flourishing today. Eventually, for the sake of more efficient organisation, she broke away from the Mother house in London and established her own Congregation. The work of this Congregation, Franciscan Missionary Sisters of Africa (whose headquarters are at Mount Oliver, Dundalk) continues in Africa today. Their contribution to education and healthcare is incalculable. It included building two hospitals for the treatment of lepers, which was a dread disease in Uganda then.

A hundred years on we gathered in Kampala to pay tribute to those early pioneers, especially to that small band of heroes, the ones referred to in our Mill Hill folklore as "the men who walked from the coast". In the area assigned to those early missionaries there are now over fifteen well established Catholic dioceses, with their own African bishops and a majority of local clergy and a wide range of churches and educational and healthcare facilities.

As a special act of commemoration a small group, led by our own Fr. Hans Burgman, decided to replicate the walk from the coast, planning as far as possible to follow the old route of the early missionaries. It was a brave venture. The small core group was joined at various locations by other walkers to share part of the journey as a gesture of support. Although they had the advantage of modern facilities it was still a hazardous undertaking. They planned their journey of about a thousand kilometres well and arrived in Kampala on 6th September, 1995, at exactly the same hour as Bishop Hanlon and his four companions had arrived a hundred years before. We gave them a huge reception, with dignitaries of Church and State there to welcome them.

The centenary was celebrated in many ways. There was Mass of Thanksgiving in Nsambya Church. The Apostolic Nuncio gave a reception to which we were all invited. The Uganda postal service ran two commemorative stamps to mark the occasion. Many government ministers paid tribute to our work and President Museveni himself thanked our Society for the wonderful contribution our Society had made in the development of Uganda.

Chapter 28
Archbishop Wamala's kidnap ordeal

It was 11.00 o'clock on Monday morning, 3rd February 1992, a pleasant sunny day. Archbishop Emmanuel Wamala was in his office, a simple building a hundred yards or so from his residence in Rubaga, a quiet leafy suburb overlooking the city of Kampala. When not on his many pastoral journeys, the Archbishop was usually available here each morning. People came to see him with all sorts of problems and requests. Visitors varied from priests and religious coming to discuss their many diocesan responsibilities, old people looking for help or perhaps students looking for school fees. The Church tried to help people in all these circumstances and the soft-spoken Archbishop embodied that spirit of benevolence. The door of his small office was open to all.

The Archbishop was seated behind his desk as a middle aged man entered. He recalls the moment vividly: "I welcomed this gentleman and gave him a chair. He had a polythene bag in his hands and put it down. I greeted him again and asked him what he wanted. He bent down and from within the bag he produced what looked like a large hand grenade. 'This is a deadly weapon', he warned me. 'I know. I once served as a soldier under Idi Amin.' Then he added with chilling intensity, 'unless I get what I want by two o'clock today, I will kill you."

The Archbishop's long ordeal was about to begin. The man explained the situation. He had Aids and he knew how it had happened. His wife had been forced to have sex with three men who had infected her. He knew their identity, the manager of a well-known bar in the city, a barman and a customer. He had now nothing to lose and it was time to take a stand against such men. He said his name as Saidhi Bingo and he wanted these three men brought here to face punishment. He knew that the Archbishop had the ear of President Museveni, who could order these men to be arrested immediately. The President greatly respected the Archbishop and would not want him harmed. The threat was real. If his wishes were not carried out, he would kill the Archbishop. The deadline was two o'clock that afternoon.

In spite of the deadly threat the Archbishop remained calm. He pointed out that the phone in his office was just an intercom with no access to the outside world. He would write a letter and have it delivered immediately but pointed out that the President was not likely to respond to such threats. "But he must" came the reply, "Otherwise you will be dead."

The Archbishop wrote the letter and through the intercom immediately alerted his staff outside. An urgent message was sent to the President on what was happening. Tension grew among his household. Security forces were called. Armed men took up positions outside. Some soldiers disguised as priests entered but Bingo suspected their identity and one motion with his hand grenade soon scattered them out the door. Hair-brained schemes were concocted such as climbing a nearby tree and shooting the kidnapper through the window. The British High Commissioner in Kampala sent four officers. Two of these, with experience in other kidnappings, helped to calm the situation and advised to play for time.

The setting for this drama was simple. The office has one door and a heavily barred window. At the back of the office was a small toilet. The kidnapper made sure the Archbishop sat behind his desk well away from the door and he himself took up a commanding position. The Archbishop tried to build up a relationship with his captor. Saidhi Bingo had once been a Christian but became a Muslin on joining Amin's army. He had nothing against the Archbishop. In fact, he greatly respected him but sadly he would have to kill him if he didn't get his way. Meanwhile the Archbishop could continue to receive visitors. One of these was a young girl asking for help as her family could not pay her school fees. As the Archbishop gently told her to come back later the captor weighed in and offered to help and gave her a small sum of money. Others came and went. One messenger spoke of the difficulty of contacting the President and pleaded for more time. The deadline was extended to eight o'clock that evening. After more discussion the deadline was extended to eight o'clock the next morning but that was final. During all this time the captor sat there with his deadly weapon ready to strike at any attempted rescue.

The evening came and went and the long night began. Some food was brought. Saidhi would just take liquid from a sealed bottle. Understandably there was little appetite for food. A blanket was brought in. The Archbishop could make himself comfortable. His captor remained alert, sitting just a couple of paces away. There would be little sleep that night.

The early morning dawned. The Archbishop realised that the end might be near as his captor was looking more strained than ever. Later he told me that far from panicking he prayed and a great calm came over him. He wrote letters, some personal, some instructive, some informative. He then asked Saidhi for permission to say Mass. Certainly, no problem. A Sister brought in the vestments, the sacred vessels, the bread and wine and the desk became an altar. The Sister served the Mass.

Saidhi had been a Catholic and so he followed the prayers and even joined in some of the responses including the Our Father. The tragic irony of the situation could not have been greater. Do you offer the sign of Peace to a man with a bomb in his hand?

Mass ended but the deadly situation remained the same. The last deadline was approaching and Saidhi made it clear that he was going to carry out his threat if his demands were not met. At one stage he demanded that the situation and his claims be broadcast over Uganda radio. The Sister who served the Mass pleaded with him. "Let the Archbishop go. He is your friend. Let me take his place." The captor smiled grimly. "No, not you, Sister, maybe another Bishop but not you. Now you had better go."

The Archbishop was now alone with his captor. The situation was getting more tense. Saidhi was tired and seemed a bit confused. With the grenade in his right hand, anything could happen. The intercom phone rang. It was a call from one of the security men. In whispered tones he told the Archbishop that something would have to be done soon so he must listen carefully. In a short while a nurse would enter and talk to Saidhi. In fact she was a trained police woman who would try to persuade Saidhi to give up. If that failed, as it probably would, as she crossed the threshold on her way out, the Archbishop should start counting. After exactly thirty seconds, he should hurl himself on the floor behind the desk as security launched an attack. It was unclear how but the moment of truth was at hand.

Then a strange thing happened. The only annexe to the office was a small toilet at the back. Whenever Saidhi used it he would first lock the office door and pocket the key. The windows were barred so there was no escape possible. Now Saidhi wished to use the toilet again and he moved to the door and locked it as usual but strangely, this time he left the key in the lock and proceeded to relieve himself in the toilet. Tired as he was, the Archbishop spotted the situation. Rising gently from the desk, pretending to stretch himself, he made a sudden dash for the door, turned the key, opened the door and flung himself out. Too late his captor saw what was happening. He gave a shout and rushed after him but the Archbishop was safe. The security men fired a volley of shots in the air. Saidhi stood paralysed at the door. He was not shot. Security personnel tried to talk to him and promised him he would not be killed, but he must defuse the bomb and come out. He hesitated and went back in. They called after him and reassured him. He came back out and seemed to agree to surrender. Then he turned again and went back into the toilet. Suddenly there was a mighty explosion. He had blown himself up. The drama was over. Police sealed off the area. A blanket was put over the dead body. The Archbishop went to the Cathedral nearby to offer a heartfelt prayer of thanks for his safe delivery.

Just two days later I had an appointment with the Archbishop. I would gladly have postponed it but he insisted on my coming and we met at his house. The meeting concerned some Society matters and it was quickly over. He provided coffee, sat back and told me the whole story. He said he felt strengthened during the ordeal by the prayers of his friends who were aware of the situation. He knew that in the Cathedral fervent prayers were being offered for his safety. He quoted the Acts of the Apostles, chapter 12, where Peter was delivered from prison through the prayers of his disciples. No, he never felt that God had abandoned him.

Afterwards he took me over to the office to show me the scene of the drama. It was badly damaged by the explosion. The toilet area was smashed completely with blood and guts splashed all over the walls. It was a terrible sight. "Do you forgiver him?" I asked. "Totally, completely," he answered. We both bowed our heads and offered a quiet prayer for the poor man whose awful situation led him to take such drastic action and come to such a tragic end. May his troubled soul rest in peace.

In 1993 Archbishop Wamala had the great joy of welcoming Pope John Paul II to Uganda. A year later he became a Cardinal and in 2005 attended the conclave in Rome which elected Pope Benedict XVI. In 2006, well past his retirement age, this much loved pastor was able to hand over to his successor and take a well-deserved rest. He had always combined strong leadership and deep learning with a gentle charming and most courteous personality. It was a privilege to have known him and to have worked with him.

Chapter 29
H.I.V.

While malaria remains the biggest cause of death in sub-Sahara Africa, a new deadly threat struck in the early eighties in the form of Aids (Acquired Immunity Deficiency Syndrome). This is the virus which breaks down the body's health defence system. The origin of Aids remains a mystery. It seems to have surfaced in Africa and in the west coast of America at about the same time. One theory is that it was passed on from monkeys. We don't know, but we were soon aware of its devastating effects on the human body. If one has Aids when a disease strikes there is no defence system and the body just fades away. A common name for it in Uganda was 'slim'.

Aids is found in the blood and in sexual fluids and is spread mostly by sexual activity, at least eighty percent of cases in Africa by hetero-sexual relationships. It is also spread through blood contact. There is danger here for some tribes who practice circumcision and are not too careful about sterilising knives and syringes. One had to be aware of the danger of blood contact. More than once when travelling at night I came upon accident cases. I always carried a pair of gloves for such emergencies but sometimes would forget to put them on. Once I lifted a poor woman from the roadway who had been struck by a speeding car and left bleeding. I placed her into the back of my car and rushed her to the local hospital. At the time I had a couple of deep scratches on my hands which were now covered with blood. As I washed them thoroughly I said a fervent prayer to the Lord for protection. Aids can also be passed from mother to her unborn baby. If the mother is positive there is a thirty per cent chance that the baby will be affected. When someone suspected of having Aids is being medically tested there is a three months 'window' period as it takes about three months for the virus to show positive.

The spread of Aids in Uganda was very rapid. In 1983 there were 17 cases recorded. By 1995 the number had gone up to fifty one thousand. The real figure was probably twice that. Women and men in their twenties and thirties were the people mostly infected, the fathers and mothers of young families. It was estimated that one in four of women of child bearing age in Kampala were HIV positive. When parents die, it falls to the grand-parents to do what they can to look after the orphan children. Uganda achieved a certain notoriety as being the centre of the Aids epidemic. In fact it was no worse than in other African countries. In nearby Kenya they hushed up the problem in case it would affect the tourist trade.

At times of crisis people will grasp at anything. A woman in the south of Uganda claimed that the soil near her home had curative powers. The idea was that you mixed it with water and drank it. Two people with Aids claimed to have been cured. Bus loads of hopefuls came from all over. Several tons of soil went down the hatch. I do not exaggerate. The Government sent a medical team to analyse the soil. They reported a total absence of any medicinal power in the soil. Still the crowds came and some people made a good profit.

As in so many crises, our missionaries were at the forefront in helping the victims. At the Catholic hospital of Nsambya Wednesday was a special day for the Aids sufferers and their families who came for help and counselling. Dr. Miriam Duggan gave her whole time to that apostolate and was appointed by President Museveni to lead the fight. Condoms were promoted widely by pharmaceutical companies but many felt that these were not the answer for various reasons. Even when used properly they are only eighty per cent reliable. A pertinent question: would you travel on a plane with just an eighty per cent safety record? Also the easy availability of condoms can promote promiscuity.

Fidelity to one's spouse or to one's partner is the key to stopping the spread of Aids. Dr. Duggan changed the government slogan of "Love carefully" to "Love faithfully." Again and again we preached that fidelity to one's partner was crucial. One slogan ran; "Zero grazing!" Don't play away from home. A vast change of behaviour was needed and we ran programmes for youth groups emphasising this.

One of the greatest obstacles to educating people to the danger of contracting Aids is a sense of fatalism in the African psyche. Many believe that our lives are conditioned by outside forces. Africans have a deep sense of the spirit world. God is the ultimate force and it would be the height of folly not to believe in a Supreme Being. However, by and large our lives are controlled by intermediate forces such as the spirits of our ancestors or other unknown powers. Life is very much a matter of good luck or bad luck. When speaking to groups about the danger of contracting Aids I often got the answer: "Shauri ya Mungu" ("It is God's business") meaning if God wants me to get it, I'll get it. This is of course a total cop-out from personal responsibility. Again and again I hammered home the lesson, "It is not God's business; it is your business and my business". That sense of fatalism does affect the behaviour of many people who should know better. The highest incidence of Aids in Uganda when I was there was among the soldiers and among the staff and students of Makerere University. One graduate whom I knew sufficiently well to warn him about his promiscuous behaviour scoffed at my advice. When I returned from leave he was dying of full-blown Aids and sadly the one question he asked me was, "Father, who put a spell on me?" It's very hard to argue against a sense of fatalism which affects many areas of public and private life.

Chapter 30
My Guardian Angel on overtime

Some of our missionaries in Uganda lived in troubled areas and one of my prime responsibilities was the welfare of our members which entailed regular contact with them. I made a point of meeting them locally, individually and in groups. I was always impressed by their overall good spirit as they got on with the job despite many difficulties. There were a few outlets for relaxation. One was fishing. The north of Uganda was disturbed by rebel activity and we had care of some parishes there. Fr. Alois Valentin was parish priest of one near Lake Kyoga. He had a sizeable rubber dinghy with a good outboard motor and it was very pleasant to go out fishing with him and with Hans Raffeiner, another missionary from Tyrol. The target was Nile perch. These fish could grow up to two hundred pounds. The ones we caught were usually about fifty or sixty pounders. Prepared properly they provided good eating. Tilapia are also numerous in the lake.

When I came back from the '88 Chapter, I had a lot of matters on which to report and I combined our planned meeting with the members in Soroti with a short stay with Fr. Alois and a fishing trip. Bro. Hans joined us. On a beautiful sunny morning we headed out for the middle of the lake where there was a small volcanic island of rock and shrubs rising to some twenty feet above the lake. The best fishing was always around the island and there was the usual competition as to who would catch the first fish. On this occasion I think I did but we were all successful and after a couple of hours our boat was fairly full with a half a dozen Nile perch. We felt we deserved a break. We tied up beside the island and climbed the steep rocky slope till we found a smooth flat rock some twenty feet above the lake. Alois produced some cold beer and some hard Tyrolese bread. Hans decided to remain below and fish for tilapia. It was most pleasant sitting in the shade of the tall shrubs, enjoying our beer and looking down at our fine catch in the boat far below.

When it was time to leave I gathered up a few items and took a careful step downwards. Suddenly Alois shouted a warning and I swung round to see why. The ledge we had been sitting on suddenly broke loose and came right at me. It was about the size of a big television set. I had no time to dodge. The rock hit me across the legs. I was thrown backwards and downwards into the lake. My shirt was ripped open by the thorny shrubs. My hat and glasses disappeared. I was conscious of severe pain in the legs and blood pumping from one of them as I hit the water near the boat. The rock smashed into the front of the rubber dinghy. Alois and Hans rushed to pull me out of the water but I had to move carefully in case of broken bones. They slowly lifted me up. I was glad to be alive. The two side cylinders of the boat were intact so it could still float. I was lifted gently into the boat. We made our way slowly away from the island back to shore. Hans kept bailing out water. The fish floated around in the boat. I sat on the side of the boat. Alois wanted to move faster and revved up the motor and the sudden movement threw me right overboard. I remember the scene clearly, the beautiful expanse of water, the glorious sunshine, the distant shore and the passing thought that this might be my last view of mother earth. As I went under, survival instincts took over. I kicked strongly which assured me I had no broken bones and came up the other side of the boat with Alois crying out, "Chris, where are you?" They heaved me in like a sack of potatoes and we made our way slowly back . Some of the locals who had seen the incident from the shore were sure the big Musungu (European) must be dead.

They took me to the mission house which had a small medical clinic with a nurse in attendance. They laid me flat on the floor of my bedroom, stripped down to my underpants. The young African nurse started gently wiping the blood off my face and shoulders. I told her to concentrate first on the deep wound below the right knee. She cleaned it thoroughly, poured pure Detol on it to disinfect it and then asked me if she should stitch it. I agreed and she did a good job and then cleaned me up completely. I was lifted onto the bed and given a refreshing cold beer. Praise the Lord, I had no after affects, not even a nightmare. The following day I got a tetanus injection at the local hospital and proceeded to Soroti where I met my colleagues and gave my report on the Chapter while propped up in an armchair. I got a lift back to the hospital in Baluba where I recovered quickly under the gentle care of the Franciscan Sisters.

My guardian angel had to work overtime on a few more occasions especially one night in Kampala a year later. I had been invited for dinner and an overnight stay with Derek Kavanagh and his wife, who lived outside Kampala. Derek from Kilkenny was a close friend and as an engineer worked on some of our projects. I was at a meeting which went on too long. To make up for lost time, I did what I had warned many of my colleagues never to do. I took a short cut through a big industrial area of Kampala noted for robbery and violent crime. It was dark with no street lights. It had rained heavily and there were large pools of water on a rough pot-holed road. I had a Toyota station wagon and drove carefully through the first stretch of water and the second. One more, I thought, and I'll be relatively safe on higher ground. As I drove gingerly into the third pool, suddenly the whole front of the car sank into a mud hole. I remember my reaction well. I was furious with myself. How could I have been such a fool? Within seconds the car was surrounded by a group of young men. I knew there were two possibilities: they were either criminals bent on plunder in which case I'd be lucky to get away with my life or they were just mischief makers out to make a little money out of someone's misfortune. I immediately switched off the engine. The water was already in around my ankles. I opened the window a little and one of them shouted at me, "Money, money, we want money before we pull you out. Give us a hundred thousand shillings" (the equivalent of about a hundred dollars). So I was lucky but I was still so angry with myself that I shouted back, "No, first get me out of here. You must have dug that hole to entrap me. Quick, the car is still sinking." Then began a real battle of wits. "The money, the money, first give us the money". "No, not till you get me out". Four of them went to the front and lifted the car a bit and pushed it back a couple of feet. "Now pay us". "No, I'm still stuck, push more". At one stage I assured them that I would pay them but not till I was completely out of the hole. A bit later I ventured the fact that I was a priest and surely some of them were Catholics. That was good for another couple of feet. Then I accused them of digging the hole themselves and how could they treat a priest like that? "Oh no Father," said one, "We are honest people". A final heave and I was safely out. Now, what shall I do if the car won't start?. I tried the ignition. The engine sparked. That was the most beautiful sound I could possibly hear. I thanked God for those Japanese engineers who devised a sealing plan for the carburettor precisely for such situations. I gave the gang a generous sum and headed back through the city to my destination. Derek's wife, Shirley, came out to greet me. I apologised for my late arrival. I had a quick shower, a change of clothes, a lovely meal and later said a fervent prayer of thanksgiving for a narrow escape and a salutary lesson.

Chapter 31
A Lady's Insight

Our missionaries have been working in Uganda since 1895 and have contributed greatly to developments in education and healthcare. We always considered this as part of the work of evangelisation, helping out in areas especially among the poorest of the poor. The government always recognised this and our work permits and entry visas were given to us at a nominal sum. This changed under the new regime in the late eighties. Suddenly our new arrivals and those of us who needed renewal of work permits were charged a hundred dollars a year.

I went to the Government minister in charge of immigration and pointed out how grossly unfair this was to members of a Society like ours who had contributed so much to the country. He agreed with me and told me the reason for the high charge. Various American sects such as the Mormons, the Moonies, the Seventh Day Adventists and Jehovah's Witnesses were all applying to come to Uganda. Previously they were not allowed but now it was decided to let them in and charge them heavily and unfortunately we were now caught under the same umbrella. I asked him if he could do something about it and he promised to help. Some time later he published a decree that any missionary who had done twenty five years service in the country was entitled to get a Life Residence permit. This was a good concession. Some ten of our missionaries had passed the twenty five year mark. I wrote up their files and presented them to the minister and each got a Life Residence Certificate recognising their valuable contribution to the country. I thanked the minister for his help.

The following year I was back in the Immigration Office with an application for a five year renewal of a work permit for one of our men who had done twelve years in the country. From my many visits I knew the girls in the office well. I greeted one of them, Elizabeth, and put the application papers before her. She would have to process them and send them to the minister in charge. I had the five hundred dollars required. She looked at the papers for a long time and then said quietly to me, "Why don't you ask for a Life Residence permit?" Me, with my typical logical, European, measuring-tape mind, gently pointed out that the applicant had done only twelve years which was quite a bit below the twenty five required in the minister's decree. I'll always remember Elizabeth's gentle reaction. With a coy smile she leaned towards me and whispered in my ear, "Father, don't you understand us Africans yet?" I was truly amazed at her insight into my lack of cop-on! I reached towards her and gave her a gentle hug. "You have a friend for life. Please give me my papers back. I'll see you soon again."

That night I burned the midnight oil writing up the files on nineteen members of our Society who had done more than twelve years in the country, myself included. I presented them to the minister requesting Life Residence for each and all were granted with no questions asked. This saved us much expense and the Certificate was also an acknowledgement of the many years of dedicated service given by all. I might add that through all this process I was never once asked for a bribe nor did I ever give one.

The Republic of Uganda

CERTIFICATE NO. 000978   IM/ 2163/61

Certificate of Residence

This is to Certify that

FR. CHRISTOPHER PETER FOX

OF P.O. BOX 933, MBALE

DAUGHTER OF | FATHER MICHAEL FOX
SON OF | MOTHER MARY JANE MULVANY-FOX

HAS BEEN GRANTED A **CERTIFICATE OF RESIDENCE** FOR LIFE
YEARS UNDER THE LAWS OF **THE REPUBLIC OF UGANDA** AS FROM THE
DATE OF THIS CERTIFICATE.

KAMPALA,

____7TH____ day of ____SEPTEMBER____ 19 90

Permanent Secretary, Ministry of Internal Affairs

Thumbprint

Issued on the authority of
The Minister of Internal Affairs

Chapter 32
Many Happy Events
A Papal Visit

When Pope John Paul II visited Uganda in 1993 he got a huge reception from all sides. The government put a fleet of motor vehicles at the disposal of the Papal entourage. Africans love to celebrate and this was one great occasion to do so. The Pope visited many parts of the country and in his own inimitable way instructed and inspired the crowds. I was fortunate to be on the reception committee at one of the venues. The climax of the visit was the Papal Mass at the Shrine of the Uganda Martyrs at Namugongo, outside Kampala. These twenty two martyrs died for their faith around the year 1866 in the persecution of King Mwanga. They were mostly young men; some were sons of chiefs, converted to Christianity just a few years before. They refused to submit to the king's evil behaviour (debauchery) and were condemned to die in a dreadful holocaust, being burned to death slowly, to the jeers of a baying mob. The youngest was a young boy called Kitzito. His father was one of the king's executioners. He begged his son to pretend to submit and thus be free. When he refused the only mercy the poor father could give his son was to dispatch him with one blow of an axe rather than see him tortured slowly in the fire. These men were canonised by Pope Paul VI in 1964. On the blood of these martyrs the Church in Uganda flourished. Today a beautiful Shrine stands in the place where they were martyred. Their Feast Day, 3rd June, is a public holiday in Uganda and Mass in the Basilica there attracts many thousands. We knew that the occasion of the papal visit there would attract over a million people and so it turned out.

Before the big event there were many receptions for diplomats and important visitors from many countries. Ireland did not have an ambassador in Uganda at the time. We were represented by a consul, Philip Curtin, an architect who had worked on some of our projects. He contacted me to say that he had not received any invitations for the various receptions. I contacted the Papal Nuncio about this with the result that he suddenly received a flood of invitations. When he rang to thank me and asked if he could do anything for me, I had one suggestion. Access to the Shrine for the Papal Mass would be a long and tedious process. I told him to mount the Irish flag on his car, put a diplomatic sign on the window and I would sit in front as his chaplain. It worked beautifully and we were waved through every check point. The whole ceremony led by the Holy Father was very inspiring. For me it brought back memories of his visit to Ireland in 1979. Pope John Paul said Mass in other centres too and was very impressed by the African style of celebrating the liturgy. One memorable sight was the presentation of the book of the Gospels by a Karimajong warrior, carried on the back of another warrior, in full native costume.

Education

Our missionaries always placed great importance on education. They established the very first Secondary School in Uganda, Namilyango College, outside Kampala, in 1902. In the Eastern province, St. Peter's College, Tororo, was established in 1944. Run by our priests and some lay staff from U.K. it had a proud record of both academic and sporting success. Now under total African management it continued to thrive. Funds were always needed and what better way to collect some than to have a Golden Jubilee celebration of the College and use the occasion as a fund raising event. President Museveni was invited as Guest of Honour. I was invited to speak on behalf of our Society, on the history of the College and our role in education. I gave careful thought to what I would say. The event was covered by national television.

There was often the impression given that our missionary work and our education system were occasions to impose our western value system on the African people. Inevitably, because missionaries were often linked with colonial powers, this sometimes happened. I spoke of the need to avoid this and that we must appreciate all that was good in the African culture and give students a pride in their native values. I stressed that all cultures, my own included, must be examined critically in the light of the teaching of Christ. I spoke of the wider approach of mission today as an effort to deepen our understanding of the mystery of God and the mystery of creation and to discover the varied ways in which God speaks to humanity in every culture. I used the occasion to pay tribute to the founders of the College and the many priests and lay staff who had served there over the years. These included some of my close friends such as John Hughes, Charlie Young and Donald MacCulloch. The address went down well and afterwards the President thanked me. In his speech at the end he paid a glowing tribute to the work of our missionary Society in Uganda, not only in education but in many areas of development.

Ordinations

1996 also saw the ordination of the first African Mill Hill priests. As I was involved in initiating the programme of accepting candidates from mission countries into our Society, it was good to see the programme being so successful and now the first two candidates were about to be ordained. They were Ephraim Odhiambo and James Juma and both were from Kenya. Their ordination was a great occasion lasting almost five hours. There is a saying among some of the locals, "God gave the Europeans the watch; He gave us time." Later the newly ordained priests were assigned to work in one of our mission countries. At a time when candidates to our Society from European countries were becoming fewer, it was good to welcome these new members to continue our missionary apostolate.

Chapter 33
A new appointment

In early 1996 I took some time out to reflect on my future and what direction it should take. I checked in at a Jesuit Retreat House in Nairobi where I could reflect and pray with no distractions. A lot had happened since I had returned to Uganda in 1982. Returning then was one of the hardest decisions I ever made. In Ireland I had a fulfilling and reasonably high profile job working for the Hierarchy who wanted me to continue I had just celebrated the Silver Jubilee of my ordination and I felt in my bones that if I didn't go back to the missions then I'd never go back. I was thinking of South America in memory of my Dad but then I got a call from Bishop Odongo of Tororo diocese to come back to that diocese to help out with pastoral renewal, by giving retreats and courses to priests, religious and parish groups. When my Superior rang me up with the offer, I immediately said yes.

I have written already about the difficulty of settling back into Uganda where there was great political and social unrest. My first year back was saddened by the deaths of my two brothers, Tom in Ireland and Michael in New York. Still in spite of all the trouble and trauma I managed to settle in to my new life in Uganda. I was much inspired by the wonderful colleagues I worked with, the priests, brothers and sisters. Many of these had borne the burden of the day and the heat during the troubled years of Amin and were still hard at work. The ordinary people in Uganda are very kind and hospitable and all this helped me to readjust.

Now in 1996 I could look back and reflect on a rather eventful number of years during which there were some significant developments. These included the establishment of a Seminary in cooperation with three other Societies. A Formation House for our Mill Hill mission candidates was built. A central headquarters for Mill Hill in Uganda was established and a big new parish opened up. As Superior during that time I had a fair share of responsibilities but in general things worked out very well. I was the Uganda delegate at two General Chapters where the wider issues of our apostolate were examined in detail. In 1995, I celebrated the 40th anniversary of my ordination. At home in my own parish of Ballymore/Boher, Fr. Phil Smith and the parishioners could not have done more to make the occasion very enjoyable. In Uganda I celebrated with four other classmates. Having completed my time as Superior in Uganda I had handed over to my successor and was free to consider my future.

Fr. Maurice McGill, our Superior General, had once asked me if I'd be willing to come to the U.K. to take charge of our Retreat Centre at Courtfield, situated on the border of England and Wales. As a new Rector had just been appointed there, I felt this was something in the future so I easily agreed. However, the new Rector, Fr. Michael Hurley, died suddenly in June. Fr. McGill rang me to remind me of my promise and sent a letter of appointment. Rather reluctantly I began to wind up my affairs in Uganda. I was expected to take up my new responsibilities in the U.K. by 1st November, 1996.

The French have a saying that to depart is to die a little. Missionaries know the meaning of this. I've seen some colleagues say goodbye, retiring after forty or fifty years of mission work and their obvious sadness at leaving people and places they had served so well. Now it was my time to say goodbye after a much shorter period but I felt rather sad just the same. There were a number of farewell parties and tokens of appreciation. One of my nieces, Kay, from New York, had always wanted to visit me in Uganda so I told her of my new appointment and when I planned to leave. She flew out and joined me for the last month of my stay. We travelled quite a bit in Uganda and Kenya, took in the sights and visited some game parks which contained a vast variety of wild life. At Murchinson Falls, in northern Uganda, the huge Nile river pours through a narrow opening in a cliff-rock, a spectacular sight. Down river hippos and crocodiles abound. Kay has many memories of our travels and there were many funny incidents including losing a tasty sandwich to a cheeky monkey who casually grabbed it from our table as we sat outside at a game lodge.

I had often said the Sunday Mass at Our Lady of Fatima church in Jinja. On my last Sunday there I said a sincere farewell to all the congregation and thanked them for making me feel so welcome over the years. I prayed for a deepening of their Christian faith and stressed two important points. I told them that Christianity will have taken deep root among them when it will have accomplished two things, a) raised the status of women to one of equality with men and b) helped people to break free from the deep sense of fatalism which affects so many aspects of their lives. I was repeating themes which they had heard me preach on many times before.

Many women were still regarded as second and third class when it came to human rights and dignity, although they were the backbone of any community and in rural Uganda did seventy per cent of all the work.

A sense of fatalism is deeply ingrained in the African psyche. Many think that much of life is a matter of chance, of good luck or bad luck. If I have an accident, it was meant to happen. If I contract Aids because of my promiscuous behaviour it is not my fault, it is just a matter of bad luck. I had often pointed out that fatalism is a total cop-out from personal responsibility. Sometimes in confession when I asked someone why he/she did something bad, the reply often was "The devil tempted me!" One has to smile because this approach goes right back to Genesis. God challenged Adam and he blamed Eve. Eve in turn blamed the serpent and – the end of the tale – the serpent hadn't a leg to stand on! Yes, we are always looking for scapegoats.

My Mill Hill colleagues gave a beautiful farewell party at the Sailing Club on the banks of the Nile. There were speeches and presentations and I was able to thank them all for the privilege of being part of a great team for the past number of years. I felt very lonely saying goodbye but one must move on. I promised I would come back within a few years but deep down I knew I was saying goodbye to some close friends that I was unlikely to see again. One of these was Fr. George Kiyingi, a wonderful Ugandan priest who was dying of cancer. I called to see members of other Societies with whom I had worked. I said goodbye to the Bishops in whose dioceses we were working. Cardinal Wamala wrote a very warm letter of appreciation and farewell. I knew him very well and the year previously at his invitation I had given a six day retreat to the Uganda Episcopal conference, nineteen Bishops in all.

On Tuesday, 8th October, my friend Derek Kavanagh took Kay and myself to Entebbe airport and we flew to Gatwick in London. After two days in London, I went to Navan to be with my sister, Teresa, and her family. Teresa's husband, Benny, who had suffered from Parkinsons for some years, was now near the end. Surrounded by so much love and care he died at home on 16th October. I was glad to be home and be with the family during this sad time. Their home in Athlumney was always home from home for me. Benny was a truly great gentleman and a most lovable character. Gifted with a beautiful voice, he had once sung for the triumphant Meath team on their homecoming after their first All Ireland success in 1949. He had married my sister in 1951 and together they raised a family of six. Benny, together with his brothers, had run a very successful furniture manufacturing business. I officiated at his funeral where a huge crowd came to pay their respects. They came from as far away as Cork and Belfast. After the funeral I was able to spend a couple of weeks with my sister and her family to share something of their sorrow before proceeding to the U.K. to take up my new appointment.

Chapter 34
Courtfield

Our Missionary Society was founded by Fr. Herbert Vaughan in 1866. He later became Cardinal Archbishop of Westminster. The Vaughans were a distinguished family who since 1562 had a large estate in south Herefordshire near the Welsh border. They were among a small group of staunch Catholic families who refused to submit to the Protestant Reformation in England and it had cost them dearly by way of penalties, loss of property and fines. One of them, Thomas Vaughan, was born in 1601 and studied for the priesthood in France. After ordination, he returned to England, was captured, tortured and died in custody. He is rightly considered a martyr. In spite of all the unjust laws, the family through the help of good friends, many of them Protestant, had managed to retain a sizeable estate which was known as Courtfield. The worst of the penal laws ended in 1829 when Catholic Emancipation was won in the House of Commons principally through the powerful rhetoric of Daniel O'Connell, surely one of the greatest orators and statesmen of his time.

In 1830 the owner of Courtfield, John Francis Vaughan, married Louisa Eliza Rolls from nearby Monmouth. Her family later achieved fame in the motor car industry. Eliza was a very devout young woman brought up in the Anglican religion and became a Catholic. There was a private oratory in the ancestral mansion and Eliza was reputed to have spent at least an hour each day praying before the Blessed Sacrament. Her two big intentions were to have a large family and that many of them would dedicate their lives to God in the priesthood or religious life. John Francis and Eliza were the parents of thirteen children. Six of their eight sons became priests. Four of their five daughters became religious sisters, surely a unique record in the annals of the Church.

Herbert, the eldest son, was born in 1832. On reaching adulthood he could look forward to a life of considerable luxury and influence. Instead he gave up the family estate to study for the priesthood. He was ordained in 1854. Sadly his mother had passed away the year before after the birth of her youngest child. Herbert had hopes of becoming a missionary in Wales. Then his vision expanded and he decided to found a missionary Society that would evangelise territories overseas, especially in Africa and the Far East. Despite enormous difficulties he collected enough money to buy a house in Mill Hill, London, to be the headquarters of his new Society which he dedicated to St. Joseph. Over the years its members became known as the Mill Hill Missionaries.

Down the years the Vaughan family continued to flourish in Courtfield. However in 1950 because of financial problems, the owner, Joseph Vaughan, sold the ancestral home and about fifty acres of land to our Society. It was suggested that it might become a retirement home for missionaries but the location is a bit isolated for that. In the early nineteen sixties it became a formation and training centre for our Brother candidates. Workshops were built and appropriate machinery installed. At one time there were up to thirty candidates training there. Later on many of these applied their skills in the construction of buildings, in mechanics and carpentry in many mission countries. In Courtfield, the Brothers built a sizeable accommodation block for themselves. When their training was transferred elsewhere, Courtfield became a Retreat Centre. It had overnight accommodation for up to forty people. This was where I was appointed as Administrator at the end of 1996.

A Retreat Centre is a place where groups and individuals come to reflect and pray. Many are devout Christians who wish to deepen their knowledge of the faith and grow in their relationship with God. Others may be searching for meaning in life and how to make sense of the ups and downs, the joys and the sorrows of life and the many complexities that confront most people. Some may just want to get away from the daily grind of work or family pressures and see where they stand. It is not a question of avoiding responsibilities but seeing things in a wider perspective and trying to focus on the spiritual side of things. For all it is a chance to recharge one's batteries and continue life with renewed vigour. There are retreats to suit different groups and different tastes. Some retreats may be based on art or pilgrimage. Some may deal with the challenge of growing old. Some may be based of methods of prayer such as that of St. Ignatius or St. Benedict. All are intended to help the participants to cope with life and to draw strength from their Christian faith.

I arrived in Courtfield on 1st November, 1996. I took a few days to study the situation and the challenges ahead. There were plenty. A Retreat Centre if not being used is like a plane grounded. It is losing money. I saw there were no bookings till after Easter. We were getting a substantial subsidy from a central fund just to keep the place going. I felt this was a waste of Society money and determined to do something about it. Courtfield is in a beautiful location, overlooking the Wye river, well off the main road, a place of peace and quiet, ideal for a Retreat Centre.

The beauty of the Wye was praised by Wordsworth in his poem *Tintern Abbey:*

> *O sylvan Wye! thou wanderer thro' the woods,*
> *How often has my spirit turned to thee.*

I had a folder printed extolling the unique location and qualities of Courtfield and distributed copies widely. I advertised in the national retreat magazine. I wrote to many Bishops, both Catholic and Anglican and to University chaplains telling them of our facilities. I knew that if a group came, saw the location and was well treated, they would certainly come back. That proved true. Within a couple of years virtually every weekend was booked out and the

Centre paid for itself. I got many letters of thanks for the facilities provided and the great hospitality received.

Courtfield was also listed as a parish in the Archdiocese of Cardiff. The beautiful church there, dedicated to Our Lady, is over a hundred years old. We had Mass each Sunday at ten o'clock for the local parishioners with a social gathering afterwards with tea and coffee. This helped to build a fine community spirit among the parishioners. Members of the Vaughan family were prominent among them. The parish was small and I was very happy to do some pastoral work as well as conducting retreats.

My first Christmas there was memorable but for the wrong reasons. We had midnight Mass and morning Mass but after all the greetings the crowd departed. The staff and cook were on leave. My only companion in the big house was a retired colleague in his late eighties.. I followed the cook's written instructions and surprised myself at how well the turkey dinner turned out. After the meal my colleague retired and I was all alone. I washed the dishes and then wandered alone among the trees outside. After the hectic Christmas celebrations in Uganda, this was quite a change. I felt I must plan something for the future. The following year I made it known that I would welcome to Courtfield elderly people who would otherwise be alone at Christmas. Many asked to come. The catering problem was solved when one of my adopted nieces, Jacinta, the daughter of Michael Carton's brother, Joe, came from Belgium with her husband and four delightful children and took over the catering with great efficiency. The old folks loved having the children around. Everyone pitched in to help and we had a great celebration over the Christmas period. This became the pattern for every Christmas after that.

Chapter 35
Pastoral & Retreat work

I spent seven years in Courtfield and enjoyed my time there. The parish was small so I was able to help out in other neighbouring parishes. I made many friends locally and also among the priests and people of Cardiff archdiocese. However my main work was looking after the retreat Centre and welcoming the groups for weekend or longer retreats. Some of these had their own chaplain but many asked me to conduct their retreats. I had the pleasure of welcoming not only Catholic groups to Courtfield but also groups from other Christian denominations. These included Anglican and Methodists students preparing for ministry and members of the Society of Friends (Quakers), and also groups from the Russian and Greek Orthodox Churches. I was very happy to promote the ecumenical dimension of our Christian faith. In one year alone over one thousand two hundred people spent time at Courtfield Retreat Centre.

I have very definite views on the way religion is presented. Too often in the past some sermons and the way catechism was taught to children often presented a God of fear rather than a God of love. While it is always necessary to warn about sin and the occasions of sin the emphasis must always be on the power of God's redemptive love, made visible in Jesus, Our Saviour. This is the Joy of the Gospel as Pope Francis outlines in a recent beautiful document.

I have two favourite quotes which I often use just to get people thinking.

One is that some people have just enough religion in them to make them miserable!

The other is that nothing hides the face of God as much as religion meaning, of course, religion distorted by strange interpretations like those presented by fundamentalist groups such as Al Qaeda or other sects, Christian or otherwise. One of my favourite Scripture quotations with which I often introduce a retreat or sermon is from John 3;15 *God loved the world so much that He gave His only Son so that everyone who believes in Him may not be lost but have eternal life.* The image of God will always remain for us a profound mystery. The only sure guide we have is Jesus Christ. He is God's fingerprints on our human nature. He is the visible face of the invisible God. He is the Way, the Truth and the Life. I strongly believe that the total vision of our Christian faith on the meaning of life is much more beautiful, intellectually satisfying and liberating than anything offered by a secular culture or the superficial values of a consumer society.

Religion today is often treated as irrelevant in our brave new world and considered just an illusion by militant atheists. However it is a strange assumption to think that to close the door on religion is to step into a wider world. Tell me if you wish, Richard Dawkins, that my beliefs are just an illusion but please don't tell me that my vision of human life stretching beyond time and space is smaller than one which sees it ending in a handful of dust. Do you think that my belief in a divine Creator is more ridiculous than the belief that something which never was could bring itself into existence? Tell me why is there something rather than nothing. To believe that human beings are infinitely precious to God, reflect His nature which they are born to share and by grace can stretch their powers beyond their natural reach is surely infinitely more enriching than to think of them as animate slime. To reject religion is not exactly a leap into freedom. It is more like jumping into a dust bin. Genuine religion adds point and energy and nobility to life.

In presenting religion it's very important to have a balanced approach. If sometimes in the past, sin and condemnation was over emphasised, there is the danger today of going to the opposite extreme of leniency and laxity. One critic of the past said, "All Jesus really asked for was love but all the Church gave us is laws". The great spiritual writer, C.S. Lewis remarked on this attitude, "What some of us want is not so much a Father in heaven as a grand-father in heaven, a sort of senile benevolence whose only wish is for all of us to have a good time!" No, we have a Father in heaven who is passionately concerned that we live up to our responsibilities. There is nothing wishy-washy about the teaching of Jesus. It's about the cost of discipleship. It's about discipline and commitment, about courage and loyalty, about truth and beauty and about the power of His love to transform our lives.

The Millennium

The near approach of the end of the 20th century and the beginning of a new Millennium gave rise to much speculation and debate. Various parties wanted to celebrate the occasion in style. Hotels put up prices; workers doubled their demands for wages. Prices flew up. Many people cancelled their bookings and decided to stay at home. I ventured something different. I invited people to come and share the last three days of the year in reflection and prayer leading up to a big celebration on New Year's Eve. I wasn't sure if anybody would come. In the end I had to close the bookings, so many applied. People had been bored with all the hype and this was something solid and different. It proved a beautiful ending to the old millennium – looking back in thanksgiving and forward in hope, in the light of our Christian faith. Everybody enjoyed it. As the new Millennium approached we had evening Mass and afterwards we repaired to the dining room for a splendid banquet. At the stroke of mid-night we all arose. There were embraces and kisses and the singing of *Auld Lang Sine* Then we made a quick trip to the Grotto overlooking the Wye valley. It was a beautiful night. We sang a hymn to Our Lady and then the Our Father. Some days later people from across the river came to tell me that I had made their Millennium worthwhile. . I was surprised as I didn't know them.

They told me they had been sitting inside, came out to watch the fireworks, looked up towards Courtfield and heard us singing the Our Father. "It came across the valley crystal clear. It was beautiful" they said. God works in many ways. There were fireworks all round and we set off a few ourselves and felt very happy about the whole experience. I could host such a gathering only with the help of many friends. Jacinta and her family from Belgium were the chief planners of the social side. My two excellent cooks, Pat Tofield and Maggie Banks, also helped. Many others joined in.

Courtfield also provided me with the opportunity to repay some of the great hospitality and friendship I myself have experienced over the years. Since my time in Uganda, two families in particular who had worked there were very close to me, the Hughes family now based in Edinburgh and the Arthurs family now living in Devon.

Members of both families visited me from time to time. Mrs Joyce Hughes celebrated her 80th birthday with us with all her family around. Rosaleen Arthurs and some of her family often spent the Christmas period with us. It was a delight to have them. Sadly both mothers have since passed away.

The future looked bright for Courtfield. Almost every weekend for the coming year was booked. However other factors were at work which put the future of the Retreat Centre in doubt and these had to be faced early in the new millennium.

Chapter 36
A Visit to Argentina

I had once promised my Dad that I would one day visit Argentina and retrace his footsteps there. The opportunity came in 1998 when my sister, Teresa's family, offered to sponsor three of us, Teresa, Sr. Catherine and myself to go on a trip there.

Fortunately I had a colleague who could take over the Retreat Centre while I was away. There is an active Ireland-Argentina group based in Longford-Westmeath under the direction of Tom Ganley and they organise trips to Argentina. They had booked a three weeks visit from 27th October till 11th November. Through an agency in Mullingar, in conjunction with one in Buenos Aires, the tour was very well planned and we were very happy to join a party of some twenty others, most of them with family ties in Argentina.

For some time I had been in contact with our own relatives there. Two of my uncles had settled in Argentina. Alexander arrived there in1865, married Catherine Rafferty and had four sons. In 1877 he was joined by his brother, Eugene (Owen). He married Catherine Tobin in 1898. My Dad who had travelled to Argentina with Eugene in 1877, was best man at the wedding. Eugene had four children, three daughters and one son. Eugene's grandson, Denis Eugene McDonnell-Fox had been in correspondence with me and we had arranged to meet up with him and his family on our visit. Other distant cousins Thomas and Norma Fox were also in touch with us and looking forward to meeting us.

We flew from Amsterdam and touched down in Buenos Aires in glorious sunshine on the morning of 27th October. We were met and warmly greeted by Delia Moretti Hafford and her daughter Moira, who ran the Westur Travel Agency, and they made us feel really at home. A gentleman met us to take delivery of a rather unusual package, a bundle of hurleys which one of our group had brought. There is an active hurling club in Buenos Aires. We were booked into a nice hotel. Dinner that evening at La Estancia was a great introduction to Argentine cuisine, fine drinks and good service and if you ordered a plank steak, you could join the chef and see it being prepared but you'd better have a mighty appetite to tackle it! The following days were spent in sightseeing and there was plenty to see in Argentina's beautiful capital.

The tour bus took in most of the usual highlights, including Plaza del Mayo, La Boca, with its famous football stadium, Madero Port with its recycled docks and elegant shops and Recoleta, a beautiful district with its well-known cemetery. The following day we had a trip on the coastal train and a mini-cruise in the beautiful El Tigre district. Most of us went to a Tango show and dinner one night in San Telmo and really enjoyed it.

The highlight of the first week took place on 31st October. On this day was held the annual Argentine-Irish Festival. It was a great event held in Campana, about a hundred kilometres from Buenos Aires. The day began with Mass in the beautiful local church. I concelebrated Mass with Fr. O'Neill, wonderful priest who had spent all his life in Argentina. I spoke a few words at the end and told them how privileged I felt visiting a country where my father had lived for over twenty years and of which he spoke so highly. After Mass we laid a wreath at the memorial to Admiral Brown (ex Co. Mayo) who is recognised as the founder of the Argentine navy. Then we proceeded to lunch and various entertainments. There was a fantastic atmosphere all round and we from Ireland were treated as guests of honour. The meal was superb. The standard of entertainment was great. A local group called the Shepperds sang Irish folk songs. It was intriguing to see and hear young men with distinctive Latin American features belting out The Wild Rover and The Fields of Athenry. Three gauchos (South American cowboys) gave a brilliant display of horsemanship. During a break in their activities I went over to one of them and explained that my Dad rode here a hundred years ago and in his memory, could I have a ride on his horse! After some laughter, they hoisted me on to the saddle, the horse under this unusual weight started to jump, my hat blew off, the crowd cheered and I got a good photograph!

The Irish ambassador to Argentina, his Excellency Art Agnew and his wife, Sylvia, honoured us with a wonderful reception at his residence on the following Monday. This was a very pleasant surprise and we all became wine experts as we tasted the wide range available.

On the 3rd November most of our group flew up to Iguazu, on the borders of Argentina and Brazil to spend a few days there viewing the scenery, especially the spectacular Iguazu Falls. These are truly worth seeing, not quite as steep as Niagara Falls but much more varied over a wide stretch of river. We viewed them from the top and from underneath where the boat pilot pretended to drive right under the avalanche of water only to veer clear at the last moment. There were some shouts of alarm, a thorough drenching and much laughter. We had a most pleasant few days there after which I looked forward to getting back to Buenos Aires where we had arranged to meet my cousin Denis from Pergamino.

Denis McDonnell-Fox was the grandson of my uncle Eugene. He collected us and took us all the way back to his home in Pergamino, a journey of about 100 miles. We were now travelling through the land where most of the Irish immigrants settled. We passed through certain small towns which indicated this as they were called after Irish family names. Today there are almost half a million in Argentina who claim Irish descent. They are very proud of their Irish background and of their Catholic faith. The focus of the celebration of their faith is centred on a beautiful basilica dedicated to Our Lady of Lujan. The origin of this centre of pilgrimage is linked with legends and miracles. The church there is a magnificent temple built in the colonial style. It is a hundred metres long with two majestic towers a hundred and ten meters high which can be seen from vast distances across the pampas. Inside are many images of Irish saints and a beautiful chapel dedicated to Our Lady of Knock. This contains a beautiful picture of Our Lady brought out from Ireland. The church is the centre for many pilgrimages and several thousands of Irish settlers meet there on special occasions. I was delighted to worship there in a place my Dad would have known so well.

We stayed with Denis and his wife Josephine for a few days and he took us to many places. One of these was the old farm house his grandfather, Eugene, once lived in when he was a successful cattle rancher. The buildings are now in ruins but for us it was an emotional occasion because of our Dad. He had been Eugene's best man at his wedding in 1898 and had lived there with him as he prepared to return to Ireland. I sat under an old eucalyptus tree and I could just imagine my Dad riding in on his horse across the pampas to this house a hundred years before.

Fr. Michael Fox, from Castletown-Geoghegan, was another cousin of ours who had served all his priestly life, over fifty years, in Argentina and had died in the early nineties. His final parish was in Rosario and he is buried under the high altar. I said Mass there and we were invited by the local priests to stay for lunch. We heard how Fr. Michael was held in high esteem by all who knew him. He had worked among the poor and championed their rights. Some of his parish publications were considered too left wing for Peron's regime and he was once arrested and spent some time behind bars. In the presbytery there were many mementos from Ireland which he had brought out including some beautiful delft plates on the dresser. I remembered meeting him when he was on leave in Ireland in 1956 and was able to chauffeur him around. That was a special year for him. He had never lost his enthusiasm for Castletown-Geoghegan hurlers and lo and behold they won the senior county championship that year in Cusack Park and he had the privilege of throwing in the ball at the start of the game.

Denis also took us to visit the beautiful cemetery in Recoleta where my two uncles are buried, Denis's grandfather, Eugene and Eugene's brother, Alexander.

We also said a prayer at the tomb of Fr. Antonio Fahy, the great Dominican priest who had been such a father figure for the Irish and had done so much for them. His memory is held in high esteem.

Soon it was time to return to our hotel in Buenos Aires and prepare for the journey home. We exchanged endless stories with our fellow travellers, many of whom had also visited relatives. Our tour guides saw us off at the airport. We felt a touch of loneliness leaving and many expressed hopes of coming back. We had a twelve hour flight to Amsterdam, then on to Dublin. I had a couple of days rest with Teresa in Navan and then went back to Courtfield.

Chapter 37
9/11

In June of 2001 I got a phone call one evening from my nephew, Kevin Fox, my late brother, Mike's, youngest son, in New York. He was getting married in September and wanted me to come over and officiate at the wedding. The date was 15th September. Although I was very busy at the time, that was one request I could not refuse, although I told Kevin my visit would be a short one. I asked the travel agent to book me on the Tuesday before the wedding. He asked me when was I free to travel as he might get a better deal earlier. He booked me on Monday 10th September. I flew into New York that evening to a warm welcome from the family.

The next morning the awful atrocity of 9/11 occurred. I had just walked home from Mass at the local church when the horror of the event became evident. The family lived in Queens and from the top of the road one could see the twin towers as the dreadful tragedy unfolded. The sight of the falling bodies, the towers collapsing, the panic on the streets, was just too unbearable to watch. To compound the fear and dread one of my nieces, Teresa, an actuary working for an insurance company, was in the building between the twin towers. It was not hit by the planes but was destroyed nevertheless. Teresa was on the 17th floor. When the first plane struck, some thought it was a bomb but all immediately evacuated and got safely down to the ground. It was 10 o'clock before Teresa could get through on her cell phone to let her anxious mother, Peggy, and all of us know that she was safe. She had to walk home from the city and it was 6 o'clock in the evening before she reached home to a very emotional welcome. She was very fortunate on another score too. She had just changed companies and some of her former colleagues whose office was high up in one of the twin towers lost their lives in the catastrophe.

The following morning the church was packed with worshippers. Many felt that prayer was the only answer one could give, prayer of reparation for the evil done and prayers for the eternal repose of the three thousand killed. A neighbouring parish lost 37 of its members, many of them firemen. We prayed for courage and strength to see our way through the mystery of this terrible tragedy and the evil perpetrated on so many innocent victims. Why, O Lord, why? For days one could still see hideous billowing clouds of smoke and ash hanging over the city. The event really provoked the indomitable courage of New Yorkers. One could only admire the heroism of the firemen, the police, doctors and nurses and so many men and women volunteering to help. There were countless acts of generosity and kindness with everyone encouraging each other and offering support. American flags appeared on every car. I put one up myself to show my solidarity.

Although the disaster cast a dark shadow over the forthcoming wedding, the two families concerned decided to go ahead on the following Saturday as planned and not let this evil stand in the way. All planes were grounded so unfortunately overseas guests couldn't travel. This affected Michael, Kevin's own brother, who was to be groomsman. He was away in Tokyo. My two sisters, Sr. Catherine and Teresa, couldn't travel from Ireland. However, most guests could travel and on Saturday 15th September, we had two beautiful ceremonies, the Catholic wedding in the church and also because the beautiful bride, Nutan Shah, is of Indian background, a colourful Indian ceremony in the hotel. Saying a few appropriate words on such an occasion is important and one point I made to the young couple was that as they looked back on their happy day it would be difficult not to associate the date with the atrocity which had happened four days before. However, they should not dwell on the evil but rather on the resultant heroism of the American people, the countless acts of courage and generosity, the great community spirit and to build their future lives on this noble foundation.

One of the saddest and most pathetic images which we witnessed on the television in the wake of 9/11 came from far away. It was the sight of some followers of Bin Laden and even some children gloating over the massacre and shouting "Allah is great". I felt if that is their image of God, who wants such a God? A monster!

It confirmed my conviction that nothing hides the face of God as much as religion when it is distorted by hatred and bigotry. Evil is never perpetrated so forcefully and gladly as when done for a religious motive. We have to admit too that down the years terrible things have been done in the name of the Christian religion. One needs to look no further than at events in parts of our own country.

Chapter 38
Holy Land Pilgrimage

Early in the year 2000 some parishioners from Monmouth invited me to be their chaplain on a pilgrimage to the Holy Land from 6th to the 15th March. I was delighted to accept. I had been to the Holy Land twice before and was always deeply moved by the experience. As the group lived locally we were able to have two preliminary meetings in the Retreat Centre to discuss the forthcoming pilgrimage. I suggested some background reading, giving relevant passages from Sacred Scripture and showing detailed maps of our journey while in the Holy Land. There was no trouble in Israel at the time and on the 6th March we flew from Heathrow to Tel Aviv. We had a pleasant bus ride north to Galilee. We were booked into a hotel in Tiberias near the lake. From there it was easy to visit the well-known places around, including Nazareth.

At the time of Jesus Nazareth was a very poor nondescript village. People asked, 'Can anything good come out of Nazareth?' Today it is a reasonably prosperous town. Exact locations of historic places are often disputed. We celebrated our first Mass in the Basilica of the Annunciation, a beautiful church with magnificent mosaics and frescos. Legend has it that the house where Mary and Joseph lived is underneath. Nearby is a smaller church thought to be the site of the synagogue where Jesus preached his first sermon, using the well-known quote from the prophet Isaiah that he had come to bring good news to the poor, liberty to captives and to set the downtrodden free. Originally his words were accepted by the people but when he began to challenge them on some of their practices, they felt threatened and expelled him from their village.

That's when he sought refuge in Capernaum. One site in Nazareth, Mary's well, is certain because it was the only source of water in Nazareth in the time of Jesus and one could easily imagine the young boy and his mother coming here daily to draw water for their house.

Our bus tour took us to Mt. Carmel where the prophet Elijah defeated the four hundred prophets of Baal in the biblical contest of fire. We visited Cana, the site of the wedding feast. Here the nine married couples with us renewed their marriage vows. Archaeologists had excavated a large stone jar which was on display. It would be similar to one Jesus used when changing water into wine at the feast. There were six of them as the Gospel of John tells us – enough wine to last the guests a lifetime! Something extraordinary happened but the meaning of the story is spiritual. Jesus was saying

My people have a religion of petty prescriptions, cold water rituals and no joy. I have come to bring them the wine of God's loving presence, the good news of the Gospel, to pour out His love in abundance, to establish a religion of consolation, hope and joy.

The next day our bus took us along by the Sea of Galilee to the Mount of the Beatitudes. There is a beautiful Renaissance style church built at the top. Here, overlooking the Sea of Galilee and the surrounding hills, we read the Beatitudes and reflected on the incomparable beauty of the words which Jesus spoke two thousand years ago. It was easy to reconstruct the scene, an obscure teacher addressing a small rather nondescript group of men and women with no great scholarship, power or influence between them and yet those magnificent words echo and re-echo down the centuries and still challenge all our values, how it is the meek not the arrogant who inherit the earth, how it is the poor not the rich who are blessed, how mercy not vengeance is the key to life. Love your enemies, do good to those who hate you; pray for those who persecute you. Later on Calvary Jesus gave the ultimate witness to love and forgiveness.

Amidst untold agony he prayed, *"Father forgive them for they know not what they do."* In His youth Jesus had seen some awful atrocities committed by the Roman legions in the valley of Jezreel. They had once put down a rebellion with utmost cruelty and left countless corpses to rot on the crosses without removing them, as a warning to the people. Jesus always preached, *'there is another way and it is the only way to true peace and happiness.'* His sublime words are as relevant today as when He first spoke them.

As a light relief I asked for some contrasting versions drawn from the dark side of modern life. Here are a few examples:

Happy are the aggressive, they shall enjoy walking on people.

Happy are those for whom money comes first; money will be their consolation.

Happy are the violent, Satan shall call them his sons.

Happy the sex consumers; they shall never know what tenderness and true love is.

Happy are they who amass fortunes at the expense of others; theirs is the kingdom of this world.

We concluded our tour of Galilee by taking a boat ride on the lake while we read the passage from Mark 5:15 where Jesus calms the storm. We visited the region of Caesarea Philippi where Peter makes his profession of faith in Jesus and is confirmed as the rock on which the Church will be built. We visited the Jordan river at the alleged site where John baptised Jesus. We climbed Mt. Tabor, the scene of the Transfiguration of Jesus. After a very full day we returned to our hotel that evening and our thoughts turned towards Jerusalem as we would be leaving for there early next morning. That evening in the hotel I had an interesting encounter. As we mixed with other guests I joined a group of four gentlemen, pilgrims from Australia, all members of the Knights of the Holy Sepulchre. One of them asked me what diocese in Ireland did I come from and I explained that I was a priest member of the Mill Hill missionaries. One of the Aussies exclaimed that he had a cousin in that Order. He said his sister in Ireland often referred to him in her letters. What's his name, I asked. "His name is Fr. Christy Fox" he said. I had to smile. "You're talking to him" I said. There was great surprise all round. He was Brendan O'Connell, a first cousin whom I hadn't seen for forty years. I remembered him only as a boy. He had emigrated to Australia as a young man and we had never met again till this moment. As both our groups were leaving for Jerusalem early next morning, we arranged to meet there for a meal and a great reunion.

There were many interesting sights on the road to Jerusalem but it was only when we were taken to the Mount of Olives that we got our first panoramic view of the city. We looked across the Kedron valley and could see the walls of the old town, still perfectly preserved. The church built on the Mount of Olives is called Dominus Flevit (the Lord wept) to remind us of the time Jesus wept over Jerusalem, because it had rejected Him. We celebrated Mass in the church. The large window behind the altar gave a spectacular view of the city bathed in evening sunshine. Afterwards we walked down the hill to the church of All Nations. This is built beside the garden of Gethsemane. The rock in front of the altar could possibly have been the rock against which Jesus leaned during his agony in the garden before he was arrested. In the garden there are some very old olive trees, possibly two thousand years old. Did they witness the scene on that tragic night? We spent some time in quiet prayer. The famous painting by Caravaggio "The Taking of Christ" came to mind.

The Church of the Holy Sepulchre is built over the site of Calvary where Jesus was crucified and the Tomb where He was buried. Various Christian sects claim rights to part of it which creates certain tensions at times. The Catholic chapel is supposedly over the place where Jesus was disrobed and nailed to the Cross. Next to it is the Orthodox chapel where the Cross is supposed to have stood. Large pieces of rock in between the altars are supposed to show the cleft in the rock which happened in the earthquake after the Crucifixion. It was a great privilege to offer Mass in this hallowed spot. After Mass we queued up to visit the Holy Sepulchre where Jesus was buried. We kissed the large stone slab worn shiny by the touch of countless pilgrims over the centuries.

During the following days we visited many places associated with the passion and death of Jesus. After His arrest Jesus was taken to the high priest, Caiaphas, to be tried and condemned. It was in the courtyard outside that Peter was accused of being a follower of Jesus. Overcome with fear he denied it with an oath and swore repeatedly that he didn't know the man. Poor Peter. The cock crew and Peter remembered the prophesy of Jesus. He went outside and wept bitterly. On the site today there is a church called Peter in Gallicantu (Peter at cockcrow). Underneath is a dungeon where Jesus possibly spent his last night before his trial. There is access now by way of a small staircase. At the time of Jesus there was just a hole at the top through which prisoners were lowered. I spent some time in prayer in the dungeon and tried to imagine the scene. There would be sounds of jeering and ribaldry from the soldiers above, probably rats and human excrement on the floor. It was chilling. Near the site of the Last Supper is a flagstone pathway leading across the Kedron valley to the Garden of Gethsemane. An archaeologist told us it was there at the time of Jesus and that it was the only pathway then. We knelt and prayed on those flagstones once touched by the feet of Jesus as he made his way to the garden of Gethsemane on that first Holy Thursday night.

Outside the site of Pilate's house was the pavement where Jesus was scourged, crowned with thorns and mocked. Markings on the stonework depicted the type of cruel game the soldiers inflicted on prisoners. Later we followed the road to Calvary, (the via dolorosa) taking turns at carrying a wooden cross through busy streets while small traders constantly accosted us in order to sell us their wares.

It was a change the next day to take a short bus ride to Bethlehem to say Mass in the Church of the Nativity. Here again there were certain tensions between the Catholic and the Orthodox churches. We celebrated Mass while crowded into a small section, supposedly the place where the manger was. Afterwards we went outside to the Shepherds Field, where we sang the Gloria in Excelsis Deo with great gusto, spiritually in union with the choir of angels and those shepherds on that first Christmas night. We visited Masada, the famous fortress where a large group of Jews held out against the Romans in 70 A.D. and chose suicide rather than surrender. We swam in the Dead Sea nearby and some took a mud bath! On our return to Jerusalem there was time to visit the Holocaust Museum, a sober reminder of man's inhumanity to man, the antithesis of all that Jesus stood for. Some went shopping for last minute gifts and we all prepared for the journey home. Many wished we could have prolonged the pilgrimage. It was very enjoyable and spiritually refreshing. On our return one pilgrim, not a Catholic, who had come along just to accompany his wife, asked for instruction in the Faith and was baptised into the Church the following year. A couple of weeks after our return we had a reunion in Courtfield, to share reflections and exchange many photographs and recall beautiful memories.

Chapter 39
Goodbye to Courtfield

My original appointment to Courtfield came towards the end of 1996. Appointments are usually for three years, often repeated for a further three years. So in the middle of 2002 I was wondering who would replace me. Then other factors sprang up which affected the future of the Retreat Centre. Because of the decline in our numbers there were fewer personnel available to fill various positions. An important financial factor was the cost of refurbishing and updating the Centre in line with the requirements of the 1995 Disabilities Act. This act demanded that all public places such as ours must provide suitable access for people with disabilities. This would require building ramps, installing elevators and a lot of restructuring. The cost was prohibitive so the General Council decided to close Courtfield at the end of 2003. It was a pity as there were many bookings for the following year and the Centre was now paying for itself, even showing a small profit. The whole property would be put up for sale. The Vaughan family were very keen to buy back what was once part of their ancestral estate. We were anxious that they should get it but the sale of the property would have to be conducted according to the rules laid down by the Charities Commission. In the end they did buy it back and everybody was pleased.

There was widespread regret at the decision to close but most people saw it was the right one, all things considered. Our many parishioners and friends planned a farewell celebration for the Sunday, 4th January. 2004. It began with Mass led by the Archbishop of Cardiff, Most Rev. Peter Smith, with a packed congregation. He thanked Our Society for its important role in the Archdiocese and said how sorry he was to see us leave. Afterwards there were refreshments and many speeches and presentations. It was an opportunity for me to thank our dedicated staff and all who helped over the years. I said that I was genuinely sorry to be leaving. I thanked those who had given me farewell gifts. I told them that I had reservations about the wording on some cards, namely those who wished me a happy retirement. I had no intention of retiring. "At your age, why aren't you retiring?" someone asked. I pointed out that at seventy two I was just my Dad's age when he begot me. So I might be planning a new career! There was much laughter.

I looked forward to being free from Society responsibilities for some time and I planned the year ahead carefully. I had been invited to go as Chaplain on a cruise to the Caribbean during the four weeks of February. After that I planned to go back to Uganda for a month and visit my old colleagues and the places where I worked. I had already booked into a course on Celtic Spirituality at a Redemptorist Centre in Perth, Scotland during May and June. In the Autumn I planned to go to the United States to visit family and friends and to help our colleagues there with fund raising for the missions. When I returned from there I hoped to do the famed walking pilgrimage in Spain to Santiago de Compostela (The Camino). At the end of the year I would offer myself to do fulltime pastoral work in the diocese of Meath as I knew Bishop Michael Smith, a friend who had often supported me when I worked in Uganda, would welcome me to his diocese.

During my last days in Courtfield I got invitations to dinner from many families including the Vaughans. On parting from them their youngest daughter, Blanche, made me promise that if she ever got married, I would come back to officiate as I had already officiated at the wedding of her sister, Teresa.

Chapter 40
Cruising to the Caribbean

We sailed out of Falmouth on the evening of 2nd February and headed south across the Bay of Biscay towards Corona in Spain, our first port of call. The ship was called the *Van Gogh*. There were about 250 passengers aboard, mostly middle-aged couples. I was the only chaplain and my duties were relatively light, including religious services at the weekend and to be available at certain times for people requesting counselling or just needing a chat. I would say Mass daily for the Catholics if they wished. I looked forward to sailing to places where I had never been. The last time I had a long cruise was when I was going out to East Africa in 1961. The officials welcomed me on board. I was given some sea-sickness pills to take which I declined as I felt I was a good traveller. The night was very stormy and I soon paid the price as I got violently sick. I retreated to my cabin, suffered for a couple of hours, then felt better and slept soundly. The following day I was fine. I met most of the passengers, told them who I was and I felt very much at ease.

I retired early the second night looking forward to a long sound sleep. At 1.30 a.m. the phone beside my bed rang. In a bit of a sleepy daze trying to figure out where I was, I picked up the phone and asked who it was. A female voice came over the line, "I must talk to you". Quietly I said, "Do you know what time it is? I can see you in the morning." "No, I must meet you right now". "Where are you?" "In the reception area, near the information desk". "O.K. I'll be there." As I hastily dressed I wondered what was the urgent matter with the lady that required my presence. I found her in the reception area and was relieved to see another young woman at the information desk, as the place was eerily quiet at that hour of the night.

The poor woman in question was having a panic attack. She told me she had to get off the boat immediately and what could be done about it? Gradually I calmed her down, sat beside her on the couch and invited her to tell me about herself, always a good approach. She was travelling with her mother. She had a partner back home; they had two children; they planned to get married in June. "Great", I said, "tell me all about your plans, the names of your children, the date of the wedding, the number of guests, what you work at, etc." It was a good tactic. She shared a lot and gradually calmed down. I asked her if she was religious as she had called for me and not the doctor. She did not practice any religion but knew some prayers. So we prayed a bit together which usually has a calming effect. She was still trembling so I told her she could cry on my shoulder. As she clung to me I put a fatherly arm around her. An amusing thought crossed my mind: if my friends could see me now, here in the dead of night, in the middle of nowhere, with a strange woman in my arms! Soon it was time to act. I suggested that she return to her cabin and I would call the doctor, get her some sleeping pills and hopefully she would be fine in the morning. She could see me then if she needed me. I called the doctor, saw her safely back to her cabin and I felt I had earned my keep. We berthed early next morning and when I looked for her she had already left the ship. I could only pray that she would be alright and find her way home safely. The company kindly flew her sister out and she joined her mother when we stopped in the Azores.

There was a small tailpiece to the story. Two mornings later as we were having breakfast on deck and I was sitting with some passengers at the end of a long table I couldn't help overhearing a loudmouth at the top describing a dramatic scene. "The other night," he said, "there was a woman spotted acting strangely, looked very unbalanced, possibly suicidal. They sent for the Vicar. He just managed to grab her as she approached the rails to throw herself over and he rescued her just in time." Much as I enjoyed my role as Leonardo DiCaprio on the Titanic, I had to chime in and tell loudmouth that his story was not quite true. He glared at me and said, "How do you know? Who are you anyway?" I said, "I'm the Vicar you're talking about!"

The cruise proved most enjoyable. When people got to know you, many came for a chat or a word of advice on some personal matter. There was a cabaret each night with good entertainment. There was a cinema with a wide range of films so I was able to become Harry Potter literate! The weather was glorious especially as we entered the Caribbean. Our ports of call included Antigua, St. Kitts, Martinique, St. Lucia, Grenada and Barbados. There were bus tours of many of the islands with opportunities to visit many places of interest and to swim in the ocean and stroll along those glorious beaches. On board there were plenty of diversions. One could study art, dress design and calligraphy. I played bridge most afternoons.

We had one sad event on the return journey. An elderly couple had just completed a couple of rounds of the deck when suddenly the husband collapsed with a heart attack. Despite the efforts of the doctor he died within a short time. I was sent for and I did what I could to help in those circumstances, prayers for the deceased and words of sympathy and consolation for Barbara the bereaved widow whose life was now suddenly turned around.

We called at Madeira on the way home and also to Virgo in Spain. We made a bus trip to Santiago de Compestela and spent some time in the magnificent Cathedral of St. James. This was the place I was hoping to visit later in the year on pilgrimage. Then we headed to Falmouth and the end of our four week's cruise. I picked up my car at a friend's house and headed back to Courtfield and prepared for my next planned trip, a visit back to Uganda.

Chapter 41
The year 2004
Return visit to Uganda

They say you can always get the missionary out of Africa but you can never get Africa out of the missionary. When one has served there for several years the people and place become part of one's makeup. In March of 2004 I returned to Uganda on a visit after an absence of eight years. At the border the inspector curtly asked for my entry permit. When I showed him my Life Residency document, his face lit up. "Welcome back, Father, where have you been all these years?" His welcome marked the beginning of a very pleasant four weeks return visit to a country I loved despite some of the hard times we went through.

I borrowed a car and travelled widely, visiting many of the places where I had worked. It was just great meeting old friends again, including two of my classmates, Bishop Joe Willigers and Fr. Henk Vergeer, still totally involved in the apostolate. It was good to see so much progress too despite the continuing problems. The new parish at Mbikko near Jinja, started from scratch just a few years before was now flourishing. I was honoured to be asked to lead the celebration of Mass there on Easter Sunday. There was a huge congregation. Afterwards many young men and women whose school fees I had paid with help from home came to greet me. They were now in employment and doing well. There were seminarians I had helped in various ways who were now young priests. The Seminary I had helped to found now had over a hundred students. I even flew up north on a small two-seater plane to Karamoja, the most primitive part of Uganda, where some of our misssionaries were now working and doing marvellous work among the nomadic tribe. I visited Tororo where the Benedictine Sisters had a great welcome for me. Nearby was the Benedictine monastery for men, founded by Fr. John Neidegger. It was also doing well. The visit here brought back many memories of past events and adventures. When my visit was near an end I took a long bus ride to Kisumu in Kenya and as I crossed the border I wondered if I would ever see Uganda again.

A renewal course in Scotland

After I returned from Uganda I had some time in Ireland before attending a seven weeks renewal course at the Redemptorist Centre near Perth, Scotland, which began on 11th May. You might well ask why would a priest in his senior years want to do a renewal course. Perhaps the titles of some of the presentations might help to explain the reason. We had courses on Growing old gracefully, Celtic Spirituality, The Healing Ministry and other subjects. There were participants from many different countries and it was great to exchange stories of our various ministries over the years. The weekends were free to explore some of the glorious scenic locations of Scotland. I even went to Lough Ness but failed to find any monster!

Celtic Spirituality

I was particularly interested in the course on Celtic spirituality. This entailed many lectures and also a trip to the island of Iona, off the west coast of Scotland. This was made famous by St. Columba (also called Colmcille) who sailed there from Ireland with twelve companions in 563. The monastery which he founded became the hub of a group of monasteries in Scotland and the north of England. They were very influential in promoting Christianity in Scotland. St. Columba can rightly be called the Apostle of Scotland. Iona is still a great centre of pilgrimage

My interest in Celtic spirituality stemmed from my experience of growing up in rural Ireland. Many of the men and women, my own parents included, had a deep sense of the presence of God in their lives, which didn't come from any catechism lesson. It showed up frequently in daily conversation. On entering a home the visitor often said, "God bless all here." On passing a work site, "God bless the work" was a common prayer. On hearing of a death the response was "May the Lord have mercy on his/her soul." Expressions such as "With the help of God", " God between us and all harm" were in common usage. The Irish greeting *Dia dhuit* (God be with you) always evoked the following answer *Dia 's Muire dhuit* (God and Mary be with you).

The Celts were very close to nature. They had deep reverence for the earth, fire, water, the sun, the ebb and flow of tides and seasons. Nature was not just a sign of God's presence but the medium through which God spoke to them. Harmony with this natural world was essential. The Celts stressed God's role as creator of heaven and earth and as the book of Genesis tells us, all created things are good. The ancient Celts worshipped the sun. St. Patrick, who had a great knowledge of Celtic beliefs from his time in Ireland as a slave, simply Christianised this practice. He told them that the sun was also part of God's creation and let it remind them of Christ the Light of the world. He stamped the Cross on the sun which is the origin of the Celtic Cross. In many ways, Patrick took what was best in Celtic pagan culture and he reframed it in terms of the Christian Gospel. People came to accept Christianity not as a rejection of their prior beliefs but as the fulfilment of them.

The early Christian Celts never saw soul and body, spirit and matter, as diametrically opposed. There is an intimate, essential relationship between the human, the natural and the divine. For them time was not a straight line which comes to an end but a circle to be completed and death is the last celebration on our earthly journey to complete the circle. There was a healthy acceptance of death because of this. Celtic Christian spirituality is very sacramental. This perspective sees the divine in the human, the infinite in the finite, the eternal in the historical. The Anglican scholar, Archbishop Temple, pointed out that Christianity is the most avowedly materialist of all the great religions, using material things as sacramental signs. Our faith is grounded in the mystery of the Incarnation. The Word became flesh and dwelt among us. The physical reality of Jesus expresses the absolute sign of God in our world, the foundational sacrament of Christianity. It was easy for the Celts to understand how God's cleansing, healing, nourishing power is mediated through water, oil, bead, wine, touch and the laying on of hands. The great Irish poet, Patrick Kavanagh, exudes Celtic spiritually in many of his poems. For him, God is in 'the bits and pieces of every day.' Kavanagh from Co. Monaghan lived in difficult times. There was great poverty in Ireland. He had a hard life and yet his spiritual vision often shone through his writings. In his epic poem, "The Great Hunger", when describing the great hardship of rural life, he goes on to say,

> *Yet sometimes when the sun comes through a gap,*
> *These men know God the Father in a tree.*
> *The Holy Spirit is the rising sap,*
> *And Christ will be the green leaves that will come*
> *At Easter from the sealed and guarded tomb.*

Return to the U.S.A.

When the course in Scotland ended I took a short break in Ireland before going to the United States. My visits there were always most enjoyable both from the great welcome from family and friends and also from the fact that I could do some useful work for the missions by way of fund raising. Each year our Society would be allotted a certain number of parishes in different dioceses where we would be allowed to preach at all the Masses at the weekend to raise money for our mission projects. I usually preached in about seven parishes, some big, some small. I experienced great hospitality from the parish priests and the response to my appeals was usually very generous. Sometimes individuals would contact me afterwards. On one occasion a man having heard me preach about the great shortage of water in a certain area where we worked, came to me and asked, "How much does one of these bore-holes cost that can provide some water?" I told him costs varied depending on how deep we had to go but a few hundred dollars would help a lot. He told me, "My father and my father-in-law were great buddies and every weekend had a good booze-up together, although they knew when to stop. I want you to sink a bore-hole in their memory." He handed me a cheque for a thousand dollars. This was typical of so many generous donations one got from many Americans.

Apart from my brothers' families to whom I remained close, I had many cousins and friends especially in New York and New Jersey. Among them were Maureen Finklestein and Cathy Lavin. They thought it would be a great idea to have a family get-together in my honour. Cathy's father, Tommie Austin, had once given a great party for me many years before. Maureen and her husband, Harvey, hosted the party one Sunday afternoon at their lovely lakeside house in New Jersey. Over thirty relatives and friends turned up and we had a great afternoon. The generous contributions of the guests were much appreciated and later helped me to provide a lot of help to certain poor parishes in Uganda where I had worked. I told the guests some stories from my time on the missions and gave them some family background, including my Dad's early history. I remember the excitement of some of the young boys who could hardly wait to tell their school pals that one of their relations had once rode with Buffalo Bill!

Before returning to Ireland in September 2004, I paid a visit to the west coast. Our Society had a house in Los Angeles in an area near Hollywood. I had a great week there visiting many places including Universal Studios viewing the secrets of the film making industry and all its make-believe. I always wanted to visit the Grand Canyon. Fr. Pat Molloy, my host and friend suggested we go to Las Vegas and go to the Canyon from there. He had a kind benefactor who let us use her house in Las Vegas as a base. It was large and spacious with a swimming pool and we stayed there for three nights. We had a memorable trip to the Grand Canyon. It was every bit as spectacular as I had imagined. We didn't go to any show in Vegas as there was plenty of street entertainment available. I did visit some of the casinos which were very well run with soft music and free drinks and a thousand subtle ways of coaxing you to part from your money. I did splurge out on one occasion and speculated all of fifty dollars. I could hardly believe my luck when, after playing a few slot machines and a roulette table, I made an extra twenty dollars. I decided to quit when ahead. I'm sure the proprietor was happy to see me go, the last of the big gamblers!

Chapter 42
Back in Ireland

When I got back to Ireland in mid September, I still planned to go to Santiago de Compostela in Spain. The pilgrimage entails walking the last hundred kilometres to the Shrine. I planned to do it with a few friends. I had already got my walking boots and my rucksack but that's as far as I got. Our Society Superior in Ireland, Fr. Maurice Crean, welcomed me back to the Irish region as I had been working abroad for the past twenty three years. Then in his quiet friendly way told me that he was hoping I would agree to take on a new appointment at our House in Kilkenny. At first that didn't appeal to me at all but I listened carefully. Our House in Kilkenny is the centre of our mission promotion work. The Society's magazine, *St. Joseph's Advocate* is published there. It has several thousand subscribers who provide financial backing for much of our mission work. Fr. Crean, a friend of many years, in his own diplomatic way, quietly persuaded me to take on more than I had bargained for, namely, to become Rector of the House in Kilkenny, to be Secretary of the promotions team and to become editor of our magazine. So I cancelled any further plans to travel. I wrote to Bishop Smith of Meath to tell him I could not accept his kind offer to work in his diocese. In late October I headed for Kilkenny to take up my new appointment.

Although rather reluctant at first to go to Kilkenny, I soon settled in to what would be my home for the next four years. There were four other priests in the house and we formed a very happy community. I was blest with the secretarial staff I inherited. The five ladies in the office who handle so much correspondence and other office business were all most efficient and a delight to work with. Our cook was equally expert and pleasant. My predecessor, Fr. Pakie Joe Ryan was most helpful and patient in guiding my way through the computer system and the various financial tabulations. The fact that he played golf and introduced me to a few courses in the area was an added bonus. Kilkenny is a beautiful city and the people are most friendly. I soon got to like my appointment and enjoyed the work it entailed.

Our mission magazine which is issued four times a year, keeps all our readers in touch with our missionaries abroad and with our various activities at home. As editor one is always looking for suitable articles of interest, eye-catching photos and interesting anecdotes. After the magazine goes out the correspondence during the following weeks is very heavy, with people sending in donations for the missions, Mass intentions and subscriptions. The secretaries could handle the bulk of the post but there were always quite a few letters requiring personal answers and these landed on my desk. They put me in touch with many people throughout the country and abroad. I never cease to be amazed at the goodness and generosity of so many people, many of whom may not be that well off. On the missions we sometimes get substantial grants from various charitable organisations but by and large the backbone of our support is the countless small and not so small contributions from ordinary people who continue to answer the calls for help year in year out.

I had Christmas at home in Ireland that year after many years abroad. I spent it with my sister, Teresa, and her family in Navan, which was very pleasant. It was surprising to see how quickly her grand children were growing up. I was also able to visit many others including my sister, Mary Jane Carton (Maisie) and her family in Horseleap. Little did we know that this would be Maisie's last Christmas. She had recovered reasonably well from a brain haemorrhage which she had suffered some years before, was very well looked after by her daughter, Margaret who is a nurse.

However on the night of 22nd March, 2005, four days before her 83rd birthday, she quietly passed away in her sleep. Maisie was a woman of deep Christian faith, whose main concern was the welfare of her family. Hers was always a cheerful, welcoming presence. Her funeral Mass in Tubber was crowded with so many family and friends and parishioners saying farewell to a truly well beloved woman. The Mass was also one of thanksgiving for her long and fruitful life.

Her husband, Michael had died some years before. They had raised a fine family of four daughters and one son. Michael Carton was a very gifted man. Like many of his generation he had the benefit of only primary education. Yet his outlook and comprehensive views on many subjects would rival those of many a philosopher. His writing and turn of phrase were always very striking. He did much amateur drama and produced some plays. I once saw him act and I felt he could have walked on to the stage of the Abbey at any time. He was also a noted raconteur. One story is worth recalling. As a little lad he was travelling to Athlone on the train in a crowded carriage. The war of Independence was on and in the next carriage there was a group of British Black and Tans. One of the passengers called young Mike, "Hey there, gossun, I'll give you a penny if you go next door and shout 'Up the I.R.A.'" Another man offered to double the money, two pennies, big money for a young lad. He slipped into the next carriage, looked up at all the strange uniforms and shouted "Up the I.R.A." and dived back before anyone could catch him, although his shout was mostly greeted with a burst of laughter. As he would tell the story in later life he concluded, "I collected my money and don't say I didn't deserve it. Many an old IRA man got a pension for less!"

The 10th July 2005 marked the Golden Jubilee of my Ordination. There was a celebration at our House in Dublin for the Jubilarians with our immediate families. The following Friday down in Ballymore/Boher, the parish priest, Fr. Phil Smith, organised a magnificent celebration. We had evening Mass of thanksgiving in

St. Brigid's church, Boher, with refreshments and entertainment afterwards in the Community Centre, Ballymore. As Fr. Smith knew I was having a lot of visitors from overseas, he insisted on getting caterers to provide an excellent lunch for them. He ordered huge tents in case it rained. As it turned out we needed the tents to protect us from the blazing sunshine. Everything went so well and I felt very humble with the number of gifts and presentations made. In my reply I was able to express my sincere thanks for everything with deep gratitude to Fr. Smith and all who helped. There were many involved with the entertainment and the refreshments. I really appreciated the wonderful celebration. It was a true community effort. After the Jubilee celebrations and some family get-togethers it was back to work in Kilkenny.

The year 2005 ended on a very sad note for all of us. Thomas Cox, Maisie's eldest grandson, the son of Mary Frances and Tony Cox, was drowned in the Claddagh river in Galway. He was just twenty one. He had completed an honours degree at Galway University and decided to stay on for further studies. A few days before Christmas he was out with a few friends, having a drink in a local pub. Rather early he decided to go back to the flat he shared as he wasn't feeling that well. His path took him along the bank of the river. His eyesight wasn't the best. It was dark and suddenly he must have slipped and fell into the river. The shock of the cold water would have stunned him. We don't know. He just disappeared. His friends back at the flat thought he had gone home and it was a couple of days before the alarm was raised. His body was found in the river on Christmas Eve. by his uncle, Pat Carton. He was taken home to Multyfarnham and waked beside the Christmas tree. The funeral took place on 27th December. It was a heart-rending time for his father and mother, his two sisters and younger brother, for relatives and friends and indeed for all who knew him. I found it very difficult as I led the ceremonies in the church and at the graveside I tried to bring the consolation of our Christian faith into the tragic situation.

Some time later Mary Frances, Thomas' mother, wrote a reflection for the local paper which touched the hearts of many people. One can only admire her faith and courage. I quote some of it here:

"Last Christmas Thomas Cox turned Multyfarnham into Bethlehem. Crowds came from far and near, young and old, from all walks of life and backgrounds to visit Thomas and share in the ceremonies. From the moment we were told that Thomas was missing we discovered a hidden Ireland that people say is gone but we found to be very much alive. The support of the whole community was evident from the initial offers to help in the search and later expressed in flowers, food, offers of transport, accommodation, Mass cards and in endless different ways. Everybody helped, friends, neighbours and colleagues, the Sub Aqua team, St. Fintan's football club, the youth Club, the Clergy, the Gardai. Crowds came and there was plenty of room at the Inn this Christmas in Multyfarnham.

During the agonising search, family friends, the Gardai scanned the skies for signs of the whereabouts of our lost son. His Star of the East was the mobile phone mast at Mill Street in Galway. We had a time and a date of his disappearance and we scanned every C.C.T.V. camera for a definite place. On Christmas Eve at fifteen minutes past midday, Thomas' uncle found him in the river just outside the Dominican church where the Claddagh basin had held him in her arms in the centre of a bustling city. I realise that the Claddagh basin could be filled with all the tears shed by the families and friends of all our young sons and daughters who have lost their lives in recent times. I share my grief with so many others as I reflect on our own family's grief at the loss of a beloved son. Thomas had gone gently into the night. When we found him, his golden hair was bedraggled but his face was calm and peaceful. Thanks to the Gardai, the Fire service, the Mortuary in Galway University Hospital and Cons Funeral Home in Mullingar, Thomas was brought home to his family in Multyfarnham on Christmas Eve. As the coffin was placed in our front room beside the Christmas tree which he had helped to decorate, his little brother, Daniel, could still say amid the tears, "Welcome home, Thomas".

Thomas' young friends from home and from Galway stayed up all night to wake him, to pray, to exchange stories, to play his favourite music, to celebrate his young life. Many wrote their thoughts down in a little book which we will always treasure. I thought of the last time I saw Thomas, saying goodbye to him at the Molly Malone statue in Dublin. I did the tourist thing and took a photo of my four children, an everyday scene of Christmas shopping with bags and bustle and Santa smiles. Little did I know that as I closed the shutter I was closing a chapter in all our lives.

We were sustained throughout our days of grief by so many good people. Thomas loved nature, to walk the country roads at sunrise and sunset. He had a large picture of the sun in his room, so when the hearse made its way to the church on St. Stephen's Day, it drove around those roads. It is a circle. All the neighbours were out with lights and candles and soon the road was a circle of light. Whether you had a Micra or a Mercedes, a candle or a flash light, it all made up that radiant circle.

Thomas was coming home to the church where he had so often served Mass, both here and in the Franciscan Friary nearby where he loved to attend Midnight Mass every year. We decided that the Mass should be one of joy and thanksgiving, for a wonderful son, for a life which was so gifted and showed such promise, but was now sadly cut short. Yes the Gloria was sung and other appropriate hymns.

The celebrant reminded us that a flower is often picked when it is blooming its loveliest. Was that why God called our son home so soon? We can only ponder and pray within the context of our Christian faith which sustains us all at times like these and have the courage to say the prayer of Fr. Bede Jarret for all our lost ones:

'We give them back to you, O God, Who first gave them to us.
As you did not lose them in the giving, so we do not lose them in the return'.
Not as the world gives, do you give, O lover of souls,
For what is yours is ours also if we belong to you.
Life is unending because love is undying.

Chapter 43
A Visit to China

When my sister, Teresa, celebrated her 80th birthday in 2006, the family presented her with a voucher for a trip to China as one of their gifts. I was invited to accompany her for which I was very grateful. In all my travels I had never been to the Far East. The following year we set off for China. After years of self imposed isolation China was now opening up in many ways, encouraging trade and tourism. I looked forward to seeing this emerging giant at first hand. Ours was a rather up market packet, staying in the best hotels and our tours were strictly controlled. Still it was all very interesting. We flew from Paris to Beijing, were met by a courier and taken to our hotel. The next morning we met the rest of our group, mostly Americans and got ready for our first tour. Beijing is a vast metropolis. I was told a thousand new cars a day were being rolled on to the streets. An eight ring road was being constructed. No wonder the air seemed less than clear. They were preparing for the Olympics the following year and fears were expressed about the effects of air pollution on the athletes. In the long term I don't know how they will cope with the necessary measures to avoid climate change.

We visited the well known tourist attractions. The Palace Museum was formerly known as the Forbidden City. Some twenty four Chinese emperors ruled from here over a period of five hundred years. It is a huge complex containing countless works of art, reflecting rich Chinese history. This was spared during the Cultural Revolution, an abominable event which destroyed so much of Chinese culture. We walked along some of the Great Wall, a truly magnificent construction, begun centuries B.C. and completed over a period of two thousand years. The Summer Palace was originally called the Garden of Clear Ripples, an incredible combination of buildings, lakes and gardens. What about this as the name of one: the Garden of Harmonious Interests! We toured Tiananmen Square where the bloody protests were held some years before and had a group photo taken under the towering portrait of Mao. He is still revered although most of his teaching is now discarded. The communist party holds tight control but by and large China is now very much a capitalist country with possibly more millionaires than the United States. The constructions in some of the cities would rival mid-town Manhattan. In classy restaurants one could see plenty of bright young executives entertaining clients or socialising with wives or girl friends. The China we saw was very much a consumer Society although there is much poverty in many of the outlying regions.

We flew to the historical city of Xi'an. This has a history of over three thousand years and is considered one of the four most ancient capitals of the world.

About twenty five miles away are the famous terracotta warriors and horses. In 1974 a local peasant digging a well accidently unearthed what proved to be one of the greatest archaeological discoveries of all time. The huge pits uncovered under mountains of soil contained almost life sized images of eight thousand terracotta warriors and horses and almost a thousand pieces of weaponry. Laid out for viewing over a great area they are now regarded as the Eight Wonder of the World.

We saw the breeding place of pandas. Apparently these are such prized rare animals today that they are valued at over a million pounds if sold to a foreign zoo.

Our tour included a six day cruise on the Yangtze river, all the way to Shanghai. We put in at several locations, viewed attractive pagodas and castles, deep caves and much glorious scenery. However the most striking of all sites was the construction of the

Three Gorges Dam. The Yangtze is one of the largest rivers in the world and this dam had been planned for many years. Back in 1944, Dr. Savage from the U.S. did a survey even while Japanese shells were still falling in the area. Under their own experts the project got under way in the fifties. Over a million people had to be evacuated to accommodate the huge back-up of water. The resultant lake is some 175 meters deep. The vast project was still under construction. Our boat slowly negotiated its way down river through five massive locks. From the lower side of the river one could view the huge discharge of water from the seven turbines generating power for millions.

After a very pleasant cruise we reached Shanghai. I found it the most beautiful and attractive city of all, with its own character and French and British quarters. I met up with Jerome Vaughan from Courtfield who has been here some years running a property market. We attended some shows. The most memorable was an incredible performance by Chinese acrobats. I wanted to take some photos but I hardly dared take my eyes away from the performers as they went through a magnificent routine. I was not surprised the following year that China won so many gold medals at the Olympics.

This was the last stop for most of our party who flew back to the States from here. Teresa and I continued on to Hong Kong for a few more days and enjoyed the sights of that great city. People knew that their independence was being threatened by the forthcoming hand-over to China and were very anxious to preserve their democratic way of life. Here there was complete freedom of religion while in mainland China religion is now tolerated but has to be very low key. In our travels I had no opportunity to contact religious leaders. I had said Mass in my cabin or in a quiet suitable place for Teresa and for some of the group who wished to join us. In Hong Kong I contacted Fr. John McGrath, a Columban missionary from my own parish of Ballymore, ordained the same year as myself. He had a great welcome for us and on the Sunday John and I led the celebration of Mass in the Cathedral before a large congregation. I thought of the worldwide outreach of the Catholic Church. Here were two men from a little place in rural Ireland leading the celebration in the exotic land of China for people from many nations and cultures.

Chapter 44
Back to Dublin

Towards the end of 2008, I finished my tour of duty in Kilkenny and transferred to our House in Dublin. I had enjoyed my work there with the great staff and company. Kilkenny is a lovely city with real character and the people are so hospitable. My parting would not be goodbye as I would remain in touch through parish promotion work and through our magazine, *The Advocate*, for which I would continue to write articles.

Our House in Dublin is situated in Rathgar. We bought a property here in 1957 to provide accommodation for our students who were attending UCD or the Miltown Institute. The original Dartry House was once owned by the well known William Martin Murphy who also owned the *Irish Independent* and the Dublin Tram system. He was not a very popular figure with the Dublin workers when he helped to break the 1913 workers strike. We bought the house and a sizeable piece of land and built quarters for our students. Over the years it served us well. Many of the students who studied here went on to Mill Hill, London, for their theological studies and ordination.

In recent times we have had no student candidates. Our last Irish Mill Hill man to be ordained was Fr. Donie O'Connor from Kerry in 2000. So the accommodation block was closed. Over the years we had sold off some of the property. Now we had to consider our present needs, especially suitable accommodation for our retired missionaries. It was decided that we should build a house to cater for all, namely, those in administration, retired missionaries, visitors and others. By selling part of the grounds we had ample funds to build a suitable residence to meet all our needs. The result is St. Joseph's House, Orwell Park, Rathgar, where we now live. The House was formally opened in July, 2007. It is spacious and comfortable and we are well looked after. We were very lucky in the fact that we sold and built at the right time.

I came here at the end of 2008 and joined a community of about twenty others. Some were in different jobs of administration. Up to a dozen were completely retired. We formed a great community with several hundred years of mission experience between us serving God in many different parts of the world. We vary in age, temperament and background. There is a great variety of views on topics such as the church, politics, sport, national and international affairs. It's great to argue the toss at times during meals or at community gatherings. There is a healthy acceptance of the fact that we are in the p.m. of life. As I pen these few lines in the autumn of 2014 we have experienced a sobering reminder of this fact as three of our colleagues have died in the recent past.

I consider myself now as active retired. I can still help out in parish work, give retreats and I write articles for religious magazines. Since coming here I have spent four summers in the United States, making appeals in various parishes under the Missionary Co-operative plan, raising funds to aid our mission apostolate. I enjoy the work. I have always experienced great hospitality. Two years ago I was invited to Chicago by Mrs Julia Maguire, a close family friend, to officiate at the weddings of her two sons, Tom and Patrick and of her daughter, Sheila. We had some wonderful celebrations. Back home I continue to get invitations to officiate at weddings of family members and friends and it is always a pleasure to do so and also to perform baptisms. Inevitably there are a number of deaths among relatives and friends too and, however sad it's good to be present to give support and consolation to the bereaved. I thank God that now in my senior years I can still help out when needed.

My health remains good although it was hard to avoid the

negative effects of years in the tropics. I have had malaria half a dozen times but got over it. The most serious challenge came from skin cancer. It's amazing how the damage can surface many years later. It did not affect me until a few years after I returned from Uganda. Over the past ten years I've had at least a dozen operations on my legs, arms and on my head. I was fortunate to be treated by expert and dedicated surgeons, Thomas O'Reilly and Aongus Curran. So I can still keep going despite a few scars. When people ask me how I lost a bit of my left ear, I pretend that I did a few rounds with Mike Tyson! Recently a hip replacement slowed me down a bit and I'm not sure if I'll manage to get back on the golf course again. Overall as I look forward to my Diamond Jubilee in July 2015 I have a mighty lot for which to be grateful.

Chapter 45
Concluding Reflections

When I look back on my life's journey it's amazing how quickly it all passed. When you are young you are immortal with life stretching out before you in an endless line. One is excited preparing for one's first job, making new friends, looking forward to perhaps marriage or in my case ordination. Even in mid-life there is little sense of ending. When I celebrated the Silver Jubilee of my Ordination, I thought how wonderful it was to be able to look forward to at least another twenty five years. Now that I'm approaching my Diamond Jubilee, how do I feel? Have I any regrets? Would I do it all over again?

As one looks back it is natural to think of other options which are now beyond one's reach such as marriage and a different career. It would have been great to have had the companionship of a loving wife and children but that was a sacrifice I made for the sake of my missionary priesthood and I don't regret it. I never lacked close family ties, having loving parents, two great brothers and three wonderful sisters and some nineteen nephews and nieces. I remained close to them and was always proud of their various achievements.

Ireland today is a vastly changed country from the one I grew up in. We are now a confident well educated people, who play an important role in the community of nations. Sadly, increased affluence brought with it some negative consequences such as drugs and related crimes. Ireland once had the lowest rate of suicides in Europe. Now it has the highest. Is this partly because of a breakdown in the faith of the people? The role of the Church in the past was dominant and authoritarian. This had to change. The Church in Ireland today has lost a lot of credibility because of the changing times and especially because of certain clerical scandals. Granted the number involved was relatively few, but the great evil done cast a cloud over all and many good priests and religious felt betrayed.

The Church is composed of human members with all the strengths and weaknesses that that entails. Over the years it has inspired countless women and men to lives of heroic self-giving and sacrifice. Sadly it has sheltered some great sinners too. Jesus was betrayed by one of his own disciples and He died between two thieves. The Church of the future will be far more humble and at the service of the poor. As I write, we have an inspiring leader to guide us, Pope Francis, truly a gift of the Holy Spirit. Down the centuries heroes and dignitaries come and go. Yet even for non religious people the person of Jesus has an incredible attraction. Many young people who turn away from the established Church are drawn to this man by His compassion, His goodness, His utter integrity, His vision of what the world could become. We believe that this person is also the unique Son of God, Our Saviour. He is Christ the King but He doesn't need thrones or courtiers or trumpeters or the trappings of power. He needs to be enthroned in our hearts by faith, hope and love and that each of us play our part in bringing His light and love to others.

My own attitude to the many challenges of life has been one of optimism. For me the glass is always half full. One of my favourite quotes from Scripture is from St. Paul's letter to the Philippians: *"Fill your minds with everything that is true, everything that is noble, everything that is good and pure, everything that we love and honour and everything that can be thought virtuous and worthy of praise... Then the God of peace will be with you."* (Phil.4:8-9)

In following my missionary vocation it has been my privilege to work with great men and women trying to bring the message of Christ to others. For centuries countless dedicated missionaries have been involved not only in establishing the Church and preaching the Gospel but also in alleviating poverty and in promoting social justice. I have seen missionary Sisters washing the feet of lepers and treating AIDS patients long before AIDS became a world issue. Countless schools, hospitals and social centres have been established by missionaries worldwide, especially for the benefit of the poor. That work continues today. It was my privilege to play some part, however inadequate, in that great apostolate and I thank God for it all. As St. Paul puts it, *"To me this grace was given to preach to the peoples the unsearchable riches of Christ."*

Epilogue

I wrote down these few scattered memories, not from any egotistical urgings, but as a tribute to the many people who were part of my life and to foster continued interest in the great outreach of the Church and hoping that it might inspire others to follow the road I took. As the poet, Robert Frost, once wrote:

> *Two roads diverged in a wood, And I –*
> *I took the one less travelled by,*
> *And that has made all the difference.*

Having travelled widely I have had opportunities to study customs and cultures in many countries. I played Gaelic football with the lads of Boher and soccer with barefooted boys in Uganda. I have walked with saints and sinners and often found the latter to be more congenial company, being a sinner myself. I offered Holy Mass in my parents' old farmhouse in Killeenbrack and I concelebrated with the Pope in the splendour of St. Peter's Basilica in Rome. I preached in remote outstations in the bush and to some distinguished groups that included princes of the Church. Yet, despite all this, my most abiding memories take me back to the young lad trotting around the farmyard at home after my kindly old Dad.

So I sat at my desk and opened the windows of my mind and let my painted butterflies fly waltzing away, iridescent under the autumn sunshine. Now I leave my pen aside and close the album.

Owen Fox - Catherine Kearney

Born 1811, Died 1879   **Born 1826, Died 1911**

They were married in the Church of the Holy Redeemer, Ballymore, Co. Westmeath on 29th July, 1846. Owen Fox came from Loughnavalley and acquired a farm in Killeenbrack, near Killare in the barony of Rathconrath. Catherine Kearney came from Ballymore.

FOX   KEARNEY

Children	Year of birth	Baptised	Died	Other details	Married to	Children
Alexander	1847	30th July	1921 (23-9)	Emigrated to Argentina 1865	Catherine Rafferty	- Eugenio (1888) Thomas (1889) Santiago Cipriano Alexandro (1892).
Thomas	1849	13th March	1899 (15-5)	Died unmarried		
John	1851	15th May	1934 (28-7)	To Argentina returned to Ireland settled in Dysart	Peg Handibo, who died 2nd wife - Kate Leavy	- Mary - Lily, Owen, Mary Ellen, Barney, John, Teresa, Jimmy, Michael, Angela.
Mary	1852	20th Dec.	1929 (2/11)	To Argentina	Unmarried	
Brigid	1854	4th March	1937 (22-8)	To Argentina	Unmarried	
Owen	1855	29th April	1940 (24-1)	To Argentina (28-5-1877)	Catherine Tobin (1898)	- Catherine (1899), Eugenio (1900) Mary Agnes (1902), Marcela (1908).
Marcella	1856	May	as an infant			
James	1857	10th August	1940 (3-6)	To Australia (Melbourne)	Elizabeth Nielsen 1882	- James, Mary, George.
Michael	1858	12th Sept.	1958 (26-3)	To Argentina (1877) returned 1900 and settled in Killeenbrack	Brigid Scally (12-2-1906) (she died 1911) Mary Jane Mulvany (5-6-1918)	- Owen (1907), Ellen (1910), Alexander (1911) - Catherine (1919), Thomas Ashe (1920), Mary Jane (1922), Michael (1924), Teresa (1926), Christopher Peter (1931).
Ellen	1860	10th July	1932 (Sept.)		Thomas Glynn, Paddinstown, Ballynacargy.	- Catherine, Maureen, Helena, William, Annie, Owen, Thomas, Peg, Josephine.
Margaret	1861	29th Dec.	as an infant			
Margaret	1862	21st Dec.	1950		Christy Austin (Dysart)	- Mary, Patrick, Eugene, Kate, Christy, Peg, John, Tommie.
Christopher	1863	July	as an infant			
Catherine	1865	15th April	1962	To U.S.A.	Joseph Glynn (1908)	- no children.
Christopher	1868	25th January	1959	To Australia, then N.Y. settled in Glascorn	Kate Cuskelly	- Kathleen, Peter.
Ann	1869	April	as an infant			
Peter	1871	31st March	1960	To Australia, then U.S.A. settled in Churchtown	Elizabeth Leavy (1905)	- Christopher, Owen, Benny, Eilish, Peter, Kathleen, Eileen, Moira, Pearse, Kevin, Donal.
Ann	1873	27th April	1956		Owen Cowley - 1905 (Cloonagh)	- Mary, Alice, Catherine, Nellie, Marcella.

The Family Tree

The family at my Silver Jubilee 1980
Back Row: *Michael, Chris, Tom,*
Front Row: *Maisie, Catherine, Teresa*

With Pope John Paul II in Rome 1982

In Uganda 1993

1993: *Uganda, with Cardinal Wamala and Dr. Kathleen O'Sullivan.*
The stone marks the spot where the first sisters arrived in 1903.